The Mystic
Road of
Love

The Mystic Road of Love

John S. Dunne

University of Notre Dame Press
NOTRE DAME, INDIANA

Copyright © 1999 by
University of Notre Dame Press
Notre Dame, IN 46556
All Rights Reserved
Manufactured in the United States of America

Set in 10.5/13.5 Electra by The Book Page, Inc.
Printed and bound by Braun Brumfield, Inc.

Library of Congress Cataloging-in-Publication Data

Dunne, John S., 1929–
    The mystic road of love / John S. Dunne.
        p.   cm.
    Includes bibliographical references and index.
    ISBN 0-268-01445-0 (hardcover : alk. paper).
  — ISBN 0-268-01446-9 (pbk. : alk. paper).
        1. Contemplation.   2. Love—Religious aspects—Christianity.
    I. Title
    BV5091.C7D87   1999
    248.2'2—dc21   99-22330

∞ *The paper used in this publication meets the minimum
requirements of the American National Standard for Information
Sciences—Permanence of Paper for Printed Library Materials,*
ANSI Z39.48-1984.

Contents

Preface

Our life is a journey in time, and God is our companion on the way. Or that is what I have come to believe. And I've begun to realize the most precious thing in my life is the companionship of God. When you read Nietzsche's *Thus Spake Zarathustra*, you have to realize, as his translator Walter Kaufmann says, "it is the work of an utterly lonely man,"[1] a man for whom God is dead. If God is alive and is with us, on the other hand, then loneliness is not the bedrock of our lives. There is something deeper than loneliness, something like the crystal core that has been lately discovered at the heart of the earth, something of the presence of God.

"Earth's inner core is spinning freely and slightly faster than the rest of the earth," it has been said, "making it virtually a planet within a planet."[2] So it is with the presence of God in a life, I believe; God is moving freely and in God's own time with respect to our time, making God virtually a person within a person. I look close at the things that come my way, therefore, believing "things are meant" and "there are signs" and "the heart speaks" and "there is a way," four little sentences I have culled from Tolkien and that seem to spell out a vision of life as a journey with God in time. If you keep a spiritual diary, I find, it is like keeping a log, a ship's log, and it gives you a sense of being on a voyage, being on a journey in time. The things that happen then appear as events on a journey, on a voyage, and seem thus to have a meaning and to point the way. I have to wait on the heart to speak clearly, but I can be confident there is a way even when it seems there is no way.

I define my life then, simply, as a journey with God in time, and that is how I've always defined my life, ever since I began my first spiritual diary in the summer of 1968, writing "My life is a journey in time, and God is my companion on the way." Then I was about to make a lone journey all through South America, but, now, in the light and shadow of what has happened afterwards, the road ahead becomes for me, as in this book, *The Mystic Road of Love*. What I am thinking of is "the road of the union of love with God," as Saint John of the Cross calls it in his *Dark Night of the Soul*.

It is true, when I first started working on this book I had a different idea of what I was doing. I thought I was writing "an essay on personal religion." But the book changed as I wrote it into a meditation on the way of personal religion and I saw ever more clearly the way is "the mystic road of love." In "Setting Out" then, I am thinking of a poem by Wendell Berry called "Setting Out" where the opening line is "Even love must pass through loneliness." There is a great circle of love, I believe, as in the words of the old Bedouin to Lawrence of Arabia, "The love is from God and of God and towards God." And when you set out on "the mystic road of love," therefore, you enter that great circle, and you find that love does indeed pass through loneliness in coming from God and returning to God. I find it does so, and yet I find the great circle nonetheless is one of love, and the night of loneliness gives way to the steady light of companionship with God. There is companionship all along the way, I have found, like Dante being guided by Virgil on "The Way Below," and by Beatrice on "The Way Above."

I divide *The Divine Comedy* into two parts instead of three, "The Way Below," where the guide is Virgil, and "The Way Above," where the guide is Beatrice. My Virgil is that of Hermann Broch's *Death of Virgil*, and my Beatrice is Ayasofya, the figure of Holy Wisdom. My method comes of putting Wordsworth's formula, "emotion recollected in tranquillity," together with Augustine's, "our heart is restless until it rests in you." On "The Way Below" I am recollecting emotion, like Broch's Virgil on his deathbed reflecting on the poetry and truth of his life and coming to "the word beyond speech." On "The Way Above" I am passing from restlessness to rest, to repose of heart in God, like the encompassing peace I once experienced in the Ayasofya, as it is called in Istanbul, the Hagia Sophia ("Holy Wisdom"), the peace I have come to associate with the figure of Wisdom, calling her by the place name Ayasofya.

"Emotion recollected in tranquillity" is the origin of poetry, as Wordsworth says, but it is also the origin of music, I believe, and of spiritual friendship, the origin of communion and of communication. There is a letting go in recollection, a forgetting in remembering, and that is the source of the "tranquillity." Recollecting my emotions in tranquillity, I come to know the love I did not know, I remember love, the love of God. Taking the love of God, as Spinoza does, simply as joy at the thought of God, I find the love of God in my joy at the thought of being on a journey in time with God as my companion. I remember my loneliness at the thought of traveling alone through South America and my joy at the thought of being with God on the journey when I began my diary with the words "My life is a journey in time, and God is my companion on the way." So "The Way Below" for me is the way down into the roots of my feelings, where I discover loneliness and the love of God at the prospect of death, just as I did at the prospect of a lone journey.

So too, "The Way Above" for me is the way of transforming my loneliness, transforming the longing into love, into the love of

God. There is a detachment in love, I have learned, a letting go of "I and it," as Martin Buber says, to live in "I and thou." In fact, that seems to be the wisdom of love, the thing I am learning from the figure of Holy Wisdom, that in loss, when life takes us down separate roads until one day we find we are alone, it is "I and it" that is lost. There is still "I and thou," and that is what is lasting in every relationship. When we go through the loss of a friendship, we lose what we had together, the "it" of our relationship, but the "I and thou" is still there. An "it" is still there too, namely what we have with God. As I see it, therefore, it is essential for me not to give my heart to what I have with another person but to give it rather to the journey with God in time. Or better, it is essential for me to realize my heart is given to God and to the adventure with God. Then I can be heart and soul, I can be whole, in every human relationship of my life. So then "The Way Below" is the low road of "I and it," and "The Way Above" is the high road of "I and thou," where there is a passing from love as longing through love as friendship to love as of God.

On the mystic road of love, finding and losing and finding again, I am always encountering mystery which "shows itself and at the same time withdraws." This showing and withdrawing is the theme of a song I wrote for this book called "Dark Light":

> Why is it dark at night?
> —a thousand stars
> are like a thousand suns!
> Why is it dark before me,
> if your light
> shines on my path?
> I can know more
> than I can tell
> of light and darkness,
> for if your eyes open,
> there is light,
> if your eyes close,

> then there is dark,
> but light inside my heart.

The song is addressed to Ayasofya, the figure of Holy Wisdom, and I have even included here the music I composed for the song.[3] At a Buddhist-Christian dialogue hosted by the Fetzer Institute in the summer of 1996 my friend Arthur Zajonc sang the song while I played the piano. And indeed there are echoes in it of the light metaphors in his own book *Catching the Light.*[4]

I have also included at the end the lyrics I wrote before and after this book for song and dance cycles based on Herbert Read's story *The Green Child* and William Morris's story *The Well at the World's End.* I have written the lyrics in "the first voice of poetry" as T. S. Eliot calls it, the personal voice, but I have transposed them into what he calls "the third voice of poetry,"[5] that of characters in a drama, by giving them to singers in my song and dance cycles. This has at times the effect of changing mystical songs into love songs. By placing them here outside the context of the stories I have let them go back to "the first voice of poetry" and let them stand as mystical songs where the capital You is the divine You.

What I come to in the end is an insight, *all our loves are one love,* the love of God. The opening song of *The Green Child* speaks of loss and setting out on a mystic road,

> Once upon
> a time of loss
> I set out on a mystic
> road of love,

but the closing song of *The Well at the World's End* speaks of insight into love,

> We found our way
> to the world's end
> where we know
> all our loves are one love.

I want to thank those who worked with me on these two song and dance cycles, especially Indi Dieckgrafe, who did the choreography and danced, also Maureen Gill, Megan McDermott, and Lindsey Phillips, who danced, and Laura Portune, who was soprano, Julie Vodicka, alto, Jeff Cloninger, tenor, and Michael Carney, baritone and narrator for *The Well at the World's End*, which we performed on April 9 and 10, 1997, in the chapel of Lewis Hall at Notre Dame. Also again Indi Dieckgrafe, who did the choreography and danced, and Julie Steciuk and Cassie Carrigan, who danced, and Alicia Scheidler, who was Siloen (soprano), and Michael Wurtz, who was Olivero (baritone), and Kevin Dreyer, who was narrator for *The Green Child*, which we performed on November 24 and 25, 1997, in the same place. My own part was composing the lyrics and the music and playing the piano accompaniment.

Setting Out

"Once upon a time of loss I set out on a mystic road of love."[1] Those words, seventeen syllables like a haiku, I wrote as the opening lyrics of a musical interpretation of *The Green Child* by Herbert Read. They describe the experience of redefining a life after going through the loss of someone or something.

When you lose someone who is important to your life, you also lose something, the communion or communication you had, and in the absence, the opening left by loss, your life's road opens up ahead of you with a different prospect than it had, a new prospect. It may be a bleak prospect of loneliness. It may be the prospect of "a mystic road of love." I see an image of this double prospect in Tolkien's Frodo. The prospect of loneliness appears in Tolkien's poem "The Sea-Bell," which he also calls "Frodo's Dreme,"[2] really Frodo's nightmare of a voyage into loneliness and desolation. The prospect of "a mystic road of love," as I call it, appears in Tolkien's trilogy where the story ends with Frodo's voyage in the company of friends into the Far West. Both voyages, the nightmare journey of the poem and the night sea journey of the trilogy, are into the Far West, but in the one he is alone and in the other he is among friends.

There is a vision of life opening up before you all the way to death in which you are alone, as Heidegger has it in *Being and*

Time, in which you have your own death to die and therefore your own life to live, and there is a vision in which you are unalone, in which "None of us lives to himself, and none of us dies to himself."[3] Is there a choice between these two alternative visions? That is, can I choose to live in the perspective of love rather than in that of loneliness, or is it more a matter of discovery, of finding out which way life is or which way life is for me? Tolkien's Frodo certainly does not choose the loneliness of the poem, but it comes upon him against his will. On the other hand, the happy ending of the trilogy, the voyage with friends into the Far West, comes to him as a gift. "A gift I will give you," Queen Arwen tells him, ". . . in my stead you shall go . . . when the time comes, and if you then desire it."[4]

I can see how these alternative visions arise out of the cycles of storytelling, out of the story of God's withdrawal and return. Once, in storytelling, God lived among us, but then God withdrew into the distance, or in another way of putting it, we emerged as the human race and separated ourselves from other living beings. Now, at the extreme point of withdrawal, we have emerged as individuals and separated ourselves even from one another. But God returns among us as Emmanuel, "God with us," and calls us to reunion with God and with one another and with all living beings.

"We are too late for the gods and too early for Being."[5] That is how Heidegger tells the larger story, trying to separate it from the story of Christ. I see the age of the gods as the time of God's withdrawal, however, as it is seen in the traditions of African peoples. And I wonder if "Being" corresponds somehow to the reunion with God and with humans and with all living beings. The prospect of loneliness that opens before us in being "too late for the gods" is like that described in Tolkien's poem "The Sea-Bell." The poem opens with Frodo walking by the sea and seeing a boat floating in on the night tide. "It is later than late!" he exclaims, "Why do we wait?" and he leaps into the boat, crying "Bear me away!" When he arrives at the far shore, though, he finds no one. "Why do you hide? Why do none speak, wherever I go?" he cries. "Come forth all! Speak to me words! Show me a face!" He grows old, and at last he gives up. "Bent though I be, I must find the sea!" he says, "I have lost myself, and I know not the way, but let me be gone!"

Another prospect seems to open before us with the thought of being "too early for Being." If we are "too early," there is still the prospect of something beyond our loneliness. It is like the prospect described in the ending of Tolkien's trilogy. It is the happy ending for Frodo. He is to find healing. "If your hurts grieve you still and the memory of your burden is heavy," he is told, "then you may pass into the West, until all your wounds and weariness are healed."[6] It is not yet the ending for Sam, however, the other main character of the story. He is "too early." His task is wholeness. "Your time may come," he is told. "Do not be too sad, Sam. You cannot always be torn in two. You will have to be one and whole for many years. You have so much to enjoy and to be, and to do."[7] So for Sam the story ends not in sailing into the West but in coming home, and the last words of the story are his when he gets home, "Well, I'm back."[8]

Healing and wholeness can come to the same thing, nevertheless, especially when you are recovering from loss and setting out on "a mystic road of love." To be whole is to love "with all your heart, and with all your soul, and with all your might,"[9] and that is also the healing of hurts and memory, of wounds and weariness. The desolate prospect of loneliness, as in "The Sea-Bell," is a bad dream, but it arises out of something very real, our emergence and separation as individuals. The prospect of healing and wholeness, on the other hand, comes of realizing our emergence and separation is not the end of the story, of realizing we are called to reunion.

"I never *am* the Other," Heidegger insists (and Derrida echoes, "Tout autre est tout autre"),[10] and so I have my own death to die and my own life to live, and yet "None of us lives to himself," as Saint Paul says to the Romans, and "none of us dies to himself." I am in relation to others, not just in relation to myself. What is more, I am ultimately in relation with God. "If we live, we live to the Lord, and if we die, we die to the Lord," Saint Paul continues, "so then, whether we live or whether we die, we are the Lord's." This is more than autonomy, the self relating to itself, and if I follow the direction of relationship in my life, I find myself on love's road. "For to this end Christ died and lived again," Saint Paul concludes, "that he might be Lord both of the dead and of the living."[11] The perspective here is not just of life opening up before us all the way to death but of life opening up before us all the way to resurrection. If we no longer assume that death is the end and is nothingness, then we no longer see ourselves as ultimately alone but as alive to God and thus also alive to ourselves and alive to one another.

Alive! And not merely alive, but *alive to*, alive to God, alive to ourselves, alive to one another! That is the prospect of reunion. I think of Saint Augustine and his journey from his early dialogues with others to his conversations with himself in his *Soliloquies* in his thirties and on to his conversations with God in his *Confessions* in his forties. What about the rest of his life, his fifties, his sixties, his seventies? There is the late work, his *Revisions*, where he goes back over all his writings and to that extent his past life. Recollection for him always meant more than just remembrance of things past. It meant recollection of the eternal in time, getting in touch with the eternal in us, as if time were, as Plato says, "a changing image of eternity."[12] His way to God, and I find myself following it, is a way of remembering God, not forgetting all else but remembering everyone and everything and finding God in them.

Recollection means collecting your wits, coming to the point where you are able to love "with all your heart, and with all your soul, and with all your might." There is a phrase that is added in the Gospels, to love "with all your mind,"[13] and that seems especially close to the thought of gathering your wits, as if to love with all your wits. If gathering my wits brings me to the center of my being, it is from there that I am able to love with all my heart and soul. "Emotion recollected in tranquillity,"[14] Wordsworth's formula, although he is speaking simply of poetry's origin, seems to describe also love's origin, to say that love comes not simply of emotion but of recollection and of tranquillity. There is wholeness there and healing in "emotion recollected in tranquillity" and especially the healing of memories, for even painful emotions can be recollected in tranquillity, and it is especially healing, I find, to express those emotions in poetry, in lyrics and in music, for instance to sing "Once upon a time of loss I set out on a mystic road of love."

There is a story of metamorphosis that has been told both in ancient and in modern times to describe the plight of the individual who has emerged and separated from humanity. It is as if by emerging and separating from humanity, the individual has become something that is no longer human. In the modern version, Kafka's *Metamorphosis*, the individual, Gregor Samsa, becomes something like a giant cockroach. In the ancient version, Apuleius' *Metamorphoses*, the individual, Lucius, becomes an ass, but he finds salvation in the end by appealing to Isis, who is the Great Goddess.[15] There is no salvation in Kafka's story, perhaps because "We are too late for the gods and too early for Being." Recollection, nevertheless, may be our way of coming into touch both with the gods and with Being.

"The Goddess gradually retreated into the depths of forests or onto mountaintops, where she remains to this day in beliefs and fairy stories," Marija Gimbutas says at the end of *The Language of the Goddess*. "But the cycles never stop turning, and now we find the Goddess reemerging from the forests and the mountains, bringing us hope for the future, returning us to our most ancient human roots."[16] As I see it, though, our hope is in God conceived not as "he" or "she" or "it" but as "you." Our hope is in an "I and thou" with God, a reunion with God that is at the same time a reunion with one another and with all living beings. A reunion with God is a return to origin, as in the saying of the old Bedouin to Lawrence of Arabia, "The love is from God and of God and towards God."[17]

If I set out on "a mystic road of love," I am setting out on a circular path, a meridian, as it were, a great circle on earth's sphere passing through the poles. It is indeed a great circle going from God to God and passing through the present moment. If I follow the path of this great circle of love, I find myself on a journey like Dante's through another world that is also this world, at once heaven and hell. He begins "lost in a dark wood" and ends caught up in "the love that moves the sun and the other stars." I begin too, lost with a sense of loss, like his sense of having lost Beatrice; "Once upon a time of loss," and I enter too upon a great circle of love, "I set out on a mystic road of love." Also I meet figures who guide me, like Virgil, who guides Dante through hell and purgatory to the earthly paradise, and Beatrice, who guides him into the heavenly paradise. If Virgil is to be my guide too, it will be Broch's Virgil, who finds his way to "the word beyond speech."[18] There is "the language of the goddess," a language of prehistoric symbols that is indeed "beyond speech," but there is also the language of Ayasofya, as I call her, the figure of Holy Wisdom who is my Beatrice.

"Broch uses the symbol of the rainbow throughout the work," says Jean Starr Untermeyer, the translator of his *Death of Virgil*. "This iridescence, this glowing and fading and merging of color, tone and meaning, gives the book a kind of natural magic, spanning symbolically the new world that always seems to be arising out of the elements to which the existing one is being constantly reduced."[19] To me the rainbow seems an image of the love that is "from God and of God and towards God." I remember driving south once in California with a rainbow showing always on my left, in the east, driving on and on to a place called Lost Hills, and there turning west into oncoming storm and darkness. I was seeing an image of my life's journey into death accompanied by the rainbow of love.

> I can see
> the rainbow in my heart
> when all my eyes see
> is the dark.[20]

Those words, again seventeen syllables like a haiku, I wrote for the Rainbow Dance of a musical interpretation I composed of *The Golden Key* by George MacDonald. I can see the rainbow of love, the love that is from God and of God and towards God, when all my eyes see is the dark of life opening up before me all the way to death.

Often a secondary rainbow can be seen concentric with and larger and fainter than the primary rainbow, the red being on the outside edge of the primary and on the inside edge of the secondary rainbow. So it is also with love. There is divine love, the primary rainbow, and there is human love, the secondary and derivative rainbow, concentric and larger and fainter to our perception. Or so it seems to me now. I know this is the opposite of Feuerbach's view that the divine is just a reflection of the human. That stormy day when I was driving south with the rainbow always showing in the east, I sometimes could see only the spring of the rainbow-arch, only that much of the primary rainbow, but it was always very vivid. That is the way it is for me in my journey in life when life opens up before me all the way to death. Sometimes I can see the rainbow of human love, but sometimes I can see only the primary rainbow of divine love, and sometimes I can see only the spring of the rainbow-arch.

There is a reflection of sunlight inside raindrops that gives rise to the rainbow, the primary rainbow, that is, but there is a double reflection inside the raindrops of the secondary rainbow. There is something like this also in divine and human love. Our love of God is a reflection of God's love of us, but our love of one another is a reflection of our love of God and of God's love of us, a double reflection therefore. When I feel the loss of human love, when I cannot see the larger and concentric rainbow, when I can see only the inner and more vivid rainbow, I wonder about the love of God, I wonder about my relationship with God. Am I God's friend? Is God my friend? I wonder, and I call upon God, as in the Psalms. The primary rainbow is still there, for I am calling upon God, and if I am calling upon God I have a relationship with God, but the secondary rainbow is invisible to me, I am feeling the absence of human love, and that is why I feel forsaken.

Because divine love is still there, I can go on with my journey, "I set out on a mystic road of love," and I can hope as I go on to see not only the spring of the rainbow-arch but the whole rainbow of divine love and the larger and concentric and fainter rainbow of human love. I suppose that is really the issue I am grappling with here, *how to go on?* It is the question you feel when you have emerged as an individual and separated to that extent from the rest of humanity. You feel the separation, the loneliness, the loss, and you seek a way of reunion with humanity and with God. That is what personal religion is, it seems to me, the reunion of the emerged and separated individual with humanity and with God. *Personal religion is about wholeness in love.* I can see the colors of the rainbow in the words "with all your heart, and with all your soul, and with all your might." Wholeness is the entire spectrum. But how do you come to whole love? I find a method by putting Wordsworth's formula, "emotion recollected in tranquillity," together with Augustine's, "our heart is restless until it rests in you."[21] By recollecting emotion in tranquillity I go from restlessness to rest, I come to repose of heart in God, and that, I believe, is wholeness and healing.

Just as there are two parts to Dante's journey, the part where Virgil is his guide and the part where Beatrice is his guide, so too in my journey, I can see, there have to be two parts, there is the part where my life opens up before me all the way to death, where I am recollecting my life like Broch's Virgil on his deathbed, reflecting on the poetry and the truth of his life, and there is the part where I am passing from restlessness to rest, to repose of heart in God, like the peace I once experienced in the Ayasofya, as it is called in Istanbul, the Hagia Sophia ("Holy Wisdom"), the peace I have come to associate with the figure of Wisdom, calling her Ayasofya.[22]

I call the part where Virgil is guide "the way below" and the part where Ayasofya is guide "the way above":

> I lose myself
> in this dark wood of loss,
> and in the middle still
> of time's adventure
> I have met in twilight
> figures of my nightmare
> who forbid my passage
> but who disappear in the light
> —so I have found my guide
> who knows the way below,
> and if this and the otherworld
> are really only one world,
> I may find again the one
> who knows the way above.[23]

There is a saying of Heraclitus, "The way above and the way below are one and the same," or perhaps simply "The way up and the way down are one and the same." T. S. Eliot takes it as motto of his *Four Quartets*.[24] It can be my watchword too "on a mystic road of love."

It is possible, however, to recollect emotion in tranquillity without coming to repose of heart in God. I think of Marcel Proust recollecting scenes of his childhood in his essay *On Reading*.[25] He recalls not so much what he read as where he was when he was reading as a child. All the same, at the end of the essay, he imagines a reader of the Gospel of Luke reading the first chapter of the Gospel and going from reading aloud to singing when coming to the two canticles, the Magnificat and the Benedictus. So he is able to imagine a recollection that leads into repose of heart in God even if his own recollection does not go so far. It strikes me that this turning point where recollection goes over into repose of heart is the moment when words go over into music. It is the moment when recollection becomes recollection of the eternal in time. Wholeness of love seems to go with wholeness of expression, the unity of words and music, and to love "with all your might" seems to mean something like this, "And David danced before the Lord with all his might."[26]

It is this last that is the missing element for me, the full bodily expression of the love of God in dancing. When I compose song and dance cycles, I compose the lyrics and the music but I always leave the choreography to the dancer. Once when I saw Sufis dancing in a little mosque in Jerusalem, jumping really and chanting "Allah . . . Allah . . . Allah,"[27] I had the impression their way to God was a way of forgetting, of forgetting all else but God. The way I am following is a way of remembering and seeing God at work in everyone and everything. What I have to learn, it seems, is how to combine the way of remembering and the way of forgetting.

I seem unable to be caught up in love, unable to be carried away with love, and yet the love is there, "our heart is restless until it rests in you" is true for me. To love with all my heart is to love with all the restless energy of my heart, and that is an unknowing love until it becomes knowing by finding expression. To love with all my soul is to bring my heart to rest in God, something that seems to happen when I am in my center. "We all have within us a center of stillness surrounded by silence"[28] is true for me too. And how come to the center? The way is to love with all my mind, to gather my wits, to recollect emotion in tranquillity, to remember God. But I still don't know how to love with all my might, to love with my body, to dance before the Lord with all my might, to lose myself and be carried away, to walk on the way of forgetting.

Here is what I have been able to understand of the way of forgetting:

> There is a cloud that comes
> between the soul and its desire,
> unknowing all we know,
> a cloud that comes also
> between the soul and all besides,
> forgetting and not just forgetting,
> letting go of sadness rather,
> like the people I saw on the Amazon
> who cannot hold on to their sadness
> —I can hold on too well
> to my sadness when it is all
> I have of memory,
> but I know to unknow
> and I remember to forget.[29]

Taking it this way, as letting go rather than literal forgetting, I can see how it is compatible with the way of remembering.

There is only one illustration in Festugière's *Personal Religion among the Greeks*. It is a photograph of a bronze in the Louvre that he entitles "Servant of Isis" and reproduces as the frontispiece of his book. To me it seems to embody the way of remembering and the way of forgetting. It is the figure of a man in sandals, standing with his arms inside his robe, his hands holding his robe together from the inside, his face uplifted towards Someone or Something. "He felt himself loved. He loved in return," Festugière says of Lucius and Isis. "It was because of these things that he found in the contemplation of his Goddess an ineffable joy. (See our frontispiece)."[30] I see this as an image of wholeness in love.

I can see myself like this in relation to Ayasofya, the figure of Holy Wisdom. In consciously personifying Holy Wisdom, I am relating to God with a conscious unknowing, knowing I do not know—this is "the cloud of unknowing." And being heart and soul in the relationship, I am letting go of everyone and everything else—this is "the cloud of forgetting."[31] There is a phrase discussed by Emmanuel Levinas, "to love the Torah more than God,"[32] a religious response to the Holocaust. To me it seems that if you love "with all your heart, and with all your soul, and with all your might," it is God you love. So too in a human relationship, if you are heart and soul in it, the human relation becomes transparently a relation with God.

When I am feeling loss in human relations, I am feeling trapped in my own story of emergence and separation as an individual. It is then, it is now that I must enter upon the larger story of reunion with humanity and with God. It is then, "Once upon a time of loss," it is now, "I set out on a mystic road of love." My life then, my life now, is about learning to love with all my heart, and with all my soul, and with all my might. Here is the answer to my question, *how to go on.* It is *by learning to love:*

> We go down
> into the heart of earth
> to learn to love
> and be heart-free.[33]

The Way Below

"Only the serene may guide,"[1] Broch says in *The Death of Virgil*. It is true! I find it so when I am drawn out of my center of stillness, following restless desire, becoming vulnerable through loss and disappointment. I have to find my way back to my center before I can find my way. A friend of mine, after an experience of unrequited love, found peace just by being with people of simple faith, people who say *Dios quiere* as if to say "God cares."

It is when the dying Virgil is arriving at the harbor of Brindisium that Broch has Virgil thinking "Only the serene may guide," thinking it as he hears the voice of a slave boy singing. "The song led them," he says, "though not for long."[2] It is a song that leads me too: Virgil has to be serene to guide me, and I have to be serene to guide others. Here is my translation of the passage from Dante that Broch quotes at the head of his *Death of Virgil*, the passage where Virgil guides Dante out of hell into the starry night:

> My guide and I upon that hidden way
> were starting back into the world of light;
> and without any wish to pause and rest
> we climbed up, he first and then I,
> and we could glimpse some of the beauty

of the sky round in an opening, and so
at last came out and saw the stars again.[3]

These are the concluding lines of Dante's *Inferno*, and they speak
to my heart, as I come out of the pain of loss and disappointment
in life and come into the peace of presence.
A trust in God, like *Dios lo quiere*, I believe, is the thing that
allows you to pass from the pain to the peace. Suppose I take the
traditional blessing from the Book of Numbers,

> The Lord bless you and keep you:
> The Lord make his face to shine
>   upon you, and be gracious to you:
> The Lord lift up his countenance
>   upon you, and give you peace.[4]

and turn it into a personal prayer,

> O Lord, bless me and keep me;
> Let your face shine upon me,
>   and be gracious to me;
> Lift up your countenance upon me,
>   and give me peace.

I am making the step, as I pray this way, into personal religion.
I am passing from "Peace!" (*Shalom* in Hebrew, *Salam* in Arabic)
to inner peace, or to praying for inner peace. I am praying for the
peace of God in a personal relationship with God.

Inner peace comes of "remembering God" (*dikhr Allah*), I want
to say, but that can mean forgetting all else. It comes, I will say, of
a recollecting of emotion in tranquillity that becomes a recollect-
ing of the eternal in time. Or this is "the way below" I wish to
follow, the way of recollection. "I have to find my way back to my
center before I can find my way," I said. That is the paradox. "And
the way up is the way down," T. S. Eliot says echoing Heraclitus,

"the way forward is the way back."[5] I follow "the way back," there-
fore, hoping it is indeed "the way forward."

"The soul stands forever at her source"

"Oh, nothing ripens to reality that is not rooted in memory, noth-
ing can be grasped in the human being that has not been be-
stowed on him from the very beginning, overshadowed by the
faces of his youth. For the soul stands forever at her source, stands
true to the grandeur of her awakening, and to her the end itself
possesses the dignity of the beginning; no song becomes lost that
has ever plucked the strings of her lyre, and exposed in ever-
renewed readiness, she preserves herself through every single tone
in which she ever resounded."[6]

As I meditate on these words, the most striking for me in the
first part of *The Death of Virgil*, I think back in my own life, back
to early memories such as my grandfather telling stories. I can't re-
member the stories, only the situation, sitting on our front porch
in the summer with other children from the neighborhood, lis-
tening to my grandfather. Although I can't remember the stories,
I can see him telling them and us children being surprised and
scared and enchanted by them. I have an impression they were
somehow like O. Henry's stories with their surprise endings. I
wonder if those stories settled in the back of my mind where I
can't get to them but where they remain still, subtle in their influ-
ence on my life. Anyway "I wonder what sort of a tale we've fallen
into?"[7] as Sam says in Tolkien's trilogy, what sort of a tale we've
fallen into and what sort of a tale I've fallen into, maybe the sort
of tale my grandfather told.

What I have come to believe is that we are in a story of emer-
gence and separation but that we are heading toward an ultimate
reunion. There are four cycles of storytelling,[8] first the cycle where
we are in touch with God and with the other living beings of the

earth, then the cycle where we emerge as the human race and separate from the other living beings, then the cycle where we emerge as individuals and separate from one another, and last the cycle where we are reunited with one another and with God and with other living beings. I see us in the third cycle, emerged and separated individuals, but going into the fourth, heading toward reunion. No doubt it is paradoxical to say all this in a time of ethnic wars. Perhaps reunion in our story is the element of surprise ending.

I can see how ethnic wars come about if I look more closely at the second cycle of storytelling. The story of the emergence and separation of *the* human race is told, as in Genesis, usually in terms of the story of a people, the emergence and separation of *a* human race. For instance, Geronimo begins his own story with that of the world and of the Apache people. The emergence and separation of the individual, the third cycle, is set in the context of the second and the first. Saint Augustine ends his story in the *Confessions* with the larger story from Genesis.[9] Ethnic wars, if I place them in this context, look like a falling back into the second cycle of story, falling back from the loneliness of the third cycle into the togetherness of the second, the togetherness of a people, instead of moving forward into the togetherness of the fourth, the togetherness of a reunion with all.

So if "the way forward is the way back," as T. S. Eliot says, it is not the way of falling back, as in ethnic wars, but the way of recollection, as when Augustine tells his story or Geronimo his, even if the story, like Geronimo's, is one of ethnic warfare. Emotion, even hatred, is recollected in tranquillity, and tranquillity brings a soul to her source.

It is loneliness that drives us back into the togetherness of a people or forward into the togetherness of reunion. I find myself unconsciously seeking that togetherness in many things I do, seeking not so much a people or a reunion as simply company. I'm consciously realizing what was unconscious here. It would be something else, something more, to move toward reunion. I read the poetry of Saint John of the Cross, and I feel called to enter upon the spiritual adventure, the road of the reunion of love with God. As I contemplate that road, I feel the inspiration of it, but now I am more acutely conscious simply of my need for companionship in life, and I remember the words I wrote at the beginning of a diary before setting out on a lone journey through South America, "My life is a journey in time, and God is my companion on the way." I added then, "Sometimes I wish I had a human companion, visible and tangible."

Still, the peace of God is real, an inner peace that I can feel. If I can trust the peace to guide me, I can follow it into a reunion with God that is also a reunion with other human beings and really with all living beings. There is something else too I gather from storytelling, especially from Tolkien, again a kind of surprise ending. It is this, if I am willing to walk alone, I may hope nevertheless to find human companionship on my way.

I can approach death as well as life with this combination of hope and willingness. Of the loneliness we feel in the face of death, Heidegger says "The less one is in a hurry to steal away unnoticed from this perplexity, the longer one endures it, the more clearly one sees that in whatever creates this difficulty for *Dasein, Dasein* shows itself in its most extreme possibility."[10] *Dasein*, "being there," is his word for human existence. In the prospect of death, he is saying, we meet ourselves at the horizon of life. If I am willing to die, I want to say, I may hope nevertheless to live. If I am willing to be alone in the face of death, I may hope nevertheless to be unalone. There is something healing and whole about this combination of willingness and hope. I know of people who have recovered from terminal disease with this very combination of a willingness to die and a hope to live. I don't mean to imply that one will always recover, only to point to the wholeness of this attitude. To me "being there" means being heart and soul in your life. If I am willing to walk alone, I may hope likewise to find human companionship, but if I do not find it, I still do find the wholeness and the healing of "being there," of being heart and soul in my life, of being able to love.

It is a response also to loss and disappointment, to be willing to walk alone and yet to hope for companionship. If I do not regain what I have lost, I still find healing and wholeness, and my hope is essential to the wholeness. "Unless you hope, you will not find the unhoped-for,"[11] Heraclitus says, and that seems almost a formula for the surprise ending. I think also of Tolkien's words, "and you may find friends upon your way when you least look for it," and later in the story, "it was said to me that I should find friendship upon the way, secret and unlooked for. Certainly I looked for no such friendship as you have shown. To have found it turns evil to great good."[12]

I have to find my way back to my center in order to find my way / I have to hope in order to find the unhoped-for. The paradox here is one and the same."For the soul stands forever at her source, stands true to the grandeur of her awakening, and to her the end itself possesses the dignity of the beginning." When I am in my own center of stillness, then, my soul is "at her source," and my hope comes upon the unhoped-for, "the end itself possesses the dignity of the beginning." As I recollect my relationships with others in my life, I find I have to differentiate, to distinguish between the persons and my own inner images, between the loves of my life, for example, and my soul image of a kind of Beatrice, *distinguer pour unir*, "to distinguish to unite," to distinguish between person and image in order to unite or reunite person and person. If I understand the distinguishing this way, however, the uniting, the union or reunion, seems to consist simply of dwelling in my center of stillness, indwelling and relating, "I and thou," center to center of stillness.

So I find myself on "the road to I and thou,"[13] as Paul Mendes-Flohr calls the way of Martin Buber's spiritual odyssey. It seems indeed a road of reunion with God and with one another and with all living beings. There is an I and thou with God, there is an I and thou with other human beings, according to Buber, and there is even an I and thou with trees and other living beings. Buber's road is "from mysticism to dialogue." I have called my own "a mystic road of love," but it seems to me an I and thou with God, on the one hand, and with trees, on the other, is also "a mystic road of love." All the same, the element of "dialogue" may be essential for me in my effort to differentiate between persons and my own inner images. I have to go from living in the solitude of my own heart to living somehow in the dialogue of heart speaking to heart.

I have difficulty with "dialogue" when I think of the solitude of the human heart, how "we all have within us a center of stillness surrounded by silence." I have difficulty with the thought of breaking the silence. I feel rather a desire for solitude, like "the inclination to retirement"[14] Festugière describes. Or I desire a balance of solitude and communication. I notice in "The Harmony of the Gospels" that its author was very impressed with the solitary moments in the life of Jesus, noting every such time in italics, "*retirement for solitary prayer.*"[15] As I read again through Buber's I and Thou, I find an answer. I can see he thinks of solitary prayer as a communing with God, and he thinks of an I and thou with a tree as a communing with a tree. So too, then, the I and thou with other human beings is a communing, not just a communication.

Reading Don Quixote side by side with I and Thou, I can see my own way "from mysticism to dialogue" or really from living in my imagination to differentiating persons from my inner images. What I come to is not really so far from Don Quixote, I and thou with God, I and thou with other human beings, I and thou with trees and other living beings. Coming back from his first sally, though, Don Quixote says "I know who I am," and so it seems to me too, living in my imagination, "I know who I am."[16] But when I differentiate persons from my inner images, I enter into an unknowing and I have to pray, like Saint Augustine, "May I know me! May I know thee!" I have to pray thus not only in the I and thou with God but also in the I and thou with other persons and in the I and thou with trees and other beings, "May I know me! May I know thee!"

There is an answer to that prayer, according to Broch's Virgil, and it is "the word that always returns into silence."[17] If I listen to another person, if I read and reread a letter from the other, I find words always return into silence, I find words are speaking to my heart but are always returning into the silence between us. I come to know myself, I come to know the other in the word, in the silence, and in the return. There is intimacy in the word, distance in the silence, and the return of the word into silence leaves me vulnerable. What I come to know of myself and the other is our intimacy and our distance, how we are near and far. I come to know myself, though, as vulnerable. I am vulnerable to love and vulnerable to sorrow. I have to "pass over," as I call it, to know the other too is vulnerable. I have to enter with sympathy, that is, into the thoughts and feelings of the other. There are depths in this knowledge, especially if we can say, with Jacques Maritain, "God is vulnerable."[18]

If the answer to "May I know me!" can be "I am vulnerable," then, the answer to "May I know thee!" can be "God is vulnerable," and "I and thou" can be seen as essentially mutual. "God and my heart are weeping together,"[19] words from a lately discovered Grimm fairy tale, can be true for me as I grieve over loss and disappointment. I have come across some opening words of a classic Grimm fairy tale, however, that seem to raise a further question about all this, "In the old times, when it was still of some use to wish for the thing one wanted."[20] These words, the beginning of "The Frog Prince," brought me to a halt. Is it no longer of any use then to wish for the thing one wants? I don't want to conclude this from "God is vulnerable." I want to say rather that the combination of willingness and hope is of some use, willingness to go without the thing one wants, hope nevertheless to obtain the thing one wants. Of what use? That brings me to the heart of the matter, the ability to love.

It is true, as Dostoevsky saw, the ability to love depends on a willingness to go through suffering. But what of actual suffering and the damage it does? It is lack and loss and letting go that make me feel vulnerable, to love and to sorrow, but also liable to grasp at someone or something to take the place left empty by lack and loss and letting go. If we think of lack and loss and letting go as the shadows of life, there is an analogy with the role of shadows in painting. There is the shading of objects and there are the shadows cast by objects. It is remarkable that in Leonardo's time, while shading was thought essential to painting, there was a tendency to avoid the casting of shadows. Before and after that time there was much use of shadows, but Leonardo recommends "a certain amount of mist or transparent cloud to be placed between the object and the sun" so that "the outlines of the shadows will not clash with the outlines of the lights."[21] I see an analogy in our concepts of wholeness in love. There is a shading that is essential to the ability to love, that of the willingness to go through suffering, but there is a tendency to exclude the cast shadows of lack and loss and letting go.

Is it possible to love even with that part of ourselves maimed by lack and loss and letting go? For me, being vulnerable involves being liable to grasp at someone or something to fill up what is missing in my life. Using Hasidic terminology, Buber calls this "the evil inclination" (*Yezer ha-Ra*) and says we must learn to love even with the power of this inclination, "that the power of even this feeling, of even this impulse, be diverted from the casual to the essential."[22]

But how is this to be done? Again, the analogy with shadows in painting is helpful. "What is strange," E. H. Gombrich writes, "is that Leonardo, the most innovative master of chiaroscuro effects, apparently did not embody in his own paintings the varieties of shadows he had studied so meticulously in his writings."[23] On the other hand, these chiaroscuro effects are the interplay of light and shadow. Instead of separating light and shadow in a hard-edged clarity, Leonardo unites them in a chiaroscuro. So it can be with the light of love and the shadow of lack and loss and letting go, especially with letting go, where lack and loss become willing rather than unwilling. If I add then the element of hope, if I let go in hope rather than in despair, I come into a chiaroscuro of love. "It is by loving, and not by being loved," George MacDonald says, "that one can come nearest to the soul of another."[24] So there can be a near as well as a far, an intimacy as well as a distance, in the interplay of love with lack and loss and letting go.

What then is my hope? It is to come near to the soul of another, and that hope is no false hope, I believe, for it belongs to the nature of loving. But then I hope to come near also to my own soul, near also to my own soul image of a Beatrice, knowing it is an inner image rather than a flesh-and-blood person. "May I know me! May I know thee!" There is a peace in this! I can feel it! Coming near to my own soul, coming near to the soul of another, I enter into a peacefulness of I and thou where all my soul's feelings have a voice, where "no song becomes lost that has ever plucked the strings of her lyre, and exposed in ever-renewed readiness, she preserves herself through every single tone in which she ever resounded."

I think of "A Blue Tale" by Marguerite Yourcenar, where seven merchants from Europe go in search of sapphires on an island. They are led to a cave of sapphires by a young woman who is deaf and mute, and all of them go away with sapphires except the Irish merchant who feels compassion for the young woman, seeing her bare feet bleeding as she walks over shards. She gives him instead a blue glass pendant she wears around her neck. All the others lose their sapphires and some lose their lives too, but their drifting ship carries the Irish merchant back to Dublin. He is starving and he finds a young woman who is a blind beggar. He begs her for a crust of bread, all she has, and she gives it to him at once. He wants to give her in return the blue glass pendant, but he cannot find it. Then as she draws closer to him to share warmth in the cold "he rested his head on her ragged knees and fell asleep feeling comforted, for her right eye, though sightless, appeared somehow to be of a miraculous blue."[25]

What I find in this story is the image of an image, the soul image of a Beatrice. She is the young woman who is deaf and mute in the beginning, and in the end she is the young woman who is blind. She is magical, always somehow handicapped, an inner image, not a flesh-and-blood person, and she is the way to hidden treasure and to warmth and comfort. I differentiate between my soul image and the real persons of my life, and I feel *bereaved* of the ones who carry the image for me, and yet "feeling comforted" I am not *bereft* of the hope and peace and friendship and understanding I have found with them. Coming near my own soul, I see, is my way of coming near the soul of another. "May I know me!" is the key to "May I know thee!"

"Love's power of remembrance"

"Oh, the lot of the poet! Love's power of remembrance had forced Orpheus to enter the depths of Hades, although at the same time it prevented him from going further, so that, lost in the underworld of memory, he was prematurely impelled to return, unchaste even in his chastity and rent in his calamity. He, unlike Orpheus, he, loveless from the beginning, unable to send forth the loving recollection and guided by no memory, he had not even reached the first level under the iron rule of Vulcan, even less the deeper realm of the law-founding fathers, and still less the much deeper one of the nothing which gives birth to the world, to memory, to salvation. He had remained in the torpid emptiness of the surface."[26]

As I read these words, the low point of *The Death of Virgil*, where Virgil feels loveless and therefore lacking in perception, I see a way past my own low point of lovelessness and imperception. It is the way implied by "love's power of remembrance": if I can love, I can remember with love, and if I can remember with love, I can love. "Loving recollection" can bring my own life to mind, my own emergence as an individual, my own lonely separation from others, but deeper than that there is the emergence and separation of the human race, "the deeper realm of the law-founding fathers," and deeper than that there is the original unity with all living beings, the realm of the mothers and the mother goddess, leading back into "the nothing which gives birth to the world, to memory, to salvation." Can I remember back so far? Or, as Rilke asks the Stranger in *Stories of God*, "Do you still remember God?"[27]

"Yes," the Stranger answers, "I still remember God," and Rilke can see in his eyes avenues of shadow leading back to a distant point of light. Yet what is it to remember God? Could it be to come upon the real as opposed to the symbolic and the imaginary? I say that because that is the way Jacques Lacan interprets the moment when Saint Thomas Aquinas says he can write no more and all he has written seems to him "like straw." That moment is similar to the low point Broch is describing when Virgil on his deathbed wants to burn the *Aeneid*. It is true, Lacan sees this simply as a moment of "subjective destitution"[28] like the end of psychoanalysis, when a person who has been in analysis has lost all illusions. But it can also be seen as a mystical encounter, as William Richardson has argued, an encounter with Someone or

Something beyond all our images and symbols. And that is the way Broch interprets Virgil's last hours, concluding "it was the word beyond speech."

It is truly a moment of "subjective destitution," I find, when you differentiate your inner images from the real persons of your life. It is like Don Quixote come back from his last sally, lying on his deathbed, stripped of his illusions. Can this too become something more "on a mystic road of love"? I find the encouragement to say "Yes" if I do not abandon the realm of the symbolic and the imaginary in trying to face the real. There is a moment in Tolkien's storytelling, for instance, when there seems to be no hope, "when Sam thought of water even his hopeful spirit quailed," but then he sees a star shining and "the beauty of it smote his heart, as he looked up out of the forsaken land, and hope returned to him." It is the sense of a universe greater than this earth that causes hope to return. "For like a shaft, clear and cold, the thought pierced him that in the end the Shadow was only a small and passing thing: there was light and high beauty forever beyond its reach."[29]

It is the thought that we are in a story larger than our own. "Don't the great tales never end?" Sam asks earlier on. "No, they never end as tales," Frodo answers. "But the people in them come, and go when their part's ended. Our part will end later—or sooner."[30] I see the great story as a journey with God and see myself on a journey with God in time, wishing at times for a human companion. I find myself falling back on this when I come up against the "real," as Lacan defines it, "what does not work." Is it enough for me to be on a journey with God, even though my part will end? Is it enough for me, though I wish at times for human companionship?

Here there is a question of focus. There is a "focus" in knowing and a "tacit dimension" in knowing, as Michael Polanyi says. When I am playing the piano, for instance, my focus is on the music and the tacit dimension is in the movement of my fingers.

It is possible to shift my attention to my fingers, and sometimes in difficult passages I do look at my fingers, but there is always a risk in doing that of losing track and interrupting the continuity of the piece. It is "the particulars" of the knowing, Polanyi says, that belong to the tacit dimension.[31] So it is here, "the particulars of my life,"[32] as Shakespeare calls them, belong to the tacit dimension while my focus is on my life as a whole, as a journey in time. So too, my wishing at times for a human companion and even my awareness that my part will end someday belong to "the particulars of my life" and to tacit awareness in knowing my life as a journey with God in time.

If "attention is the natural prayer of the soul,"[33] as Malebranche said, then it makes sense to give my attention to my life as a journey with God in time. If I give my attention to God, however, or to the journey with God, I am letting love and death play a tacit role, tacit but conscious. I am "dwelling in the particulars" of my life, dwelling in my loneliness, dwelling in my mortality, while focusing on my daily adventure with God. Perhaps this is what is meant by "letting go" and "forgetting" in the language of mysticism. If so, the things I let go do not go away, the things I forget are not forgotten. I continue to dwell in them while I have my eyes on the road, looking to God's leading in the situations I meet, trying to read the signs, waiting for the heart to speak, letting the next step become clear.

What I am coming to here, I believe, is an integrating vision, an integration of the real and the symbolic and the imaginary. It comes after the differentiation, after distinguishing my inner images from the real persons of my life. What Lacan calls "the real," namely "what does not work,"[34] is something that comes to light in the differentiation. Or then again, the encounter with "the real" leads you to differentiate it from "the symbolic" and "the imaginary." But my integration, my vision of a journey with God in time is still vulnerable to an encounter with "the real." That is just what seems to have happened in the last days of Saint Thomas

Aquinas, when his own unified worldview seemed to him "like straw," and in the last hours of Virgil, when he wanted to burn the *Aeneid*. I think of Tolstoy's Ivan Ilych on his deathbed, wanting to say *Prosti*, "Forgive," and instead saying *Propusti*, "Farewell."[35]

These are both words for "letting go," *Prosti* and *Propusti*, or for "letting be." They speak of a relationship with life and with the particulars of a life. I think of Meister Eckhart's term for "letting be," *Gelassenheit*,[36] revived by Heidegger in our times. I can see its importance when I think of phrases like "Let there be light!" At any rate "letting be" seems appropriate to me in a time of lack or of loss. I can imagine it seeming so also on the deathbed, saying "Farewell" to life. There is another attitude that is closely linked with "letting be," and that is "openness to the mystery,"[37] and that too seems appropriate to me in lack and loss, and I imagine it too on the deathbed. If "letting be" is my relationship to "the particulars of my life," then "openness to the mystery" can be my focus, like Ivan Ilych seeing "In place of death there was light."

It is by letting be, by letting the particulars of my life be, that I come to discern the mystery of my life, that I come to see the light. Letting be, as I understand it, is a loving recollection of the things of my life, a remembering that is a forgetting, a letting go, a forgetting that is a remembering, a letting be. Say I recollect my own life in this manner, using the autobiographical method of Proust in his little essay *On Reading*. Say I recollect my life, that is, by recollecting what I have read, by recollecting the circumstances of my reading, especially when reading has brought me an emotional tranquillity. Recollection here is like learning a piece on the piano: the part that is the tacit dimension, the movement of my fingers, is at first the center of attention, at least in difficult passages. Only afterward, when I have learned the piece, does it become tacit. Then my attention moves to the music as a whole. So it is here, after recollecting the particulars, I am able to come to a sense of my life as a whole.

At first I read just for enjoyment. When it was bedtime for me as a child, I was always allowed to read in bed, but if I was not reading I had to turn off the lamp and go to sleep. So for me there was always a great inducement to read, and I did read book after book, stories of all kinds, fairy tales, sea stories, and other stories of adventure. Then later I read lives. My reading had become more serious. I was reading for living. And eventually I read the lives of the saints, and I was inspired to set out on the spiritual adventure that I have been on ever since. There were especially two by G. K. Chesterton, a life of Saint Francis that spoke of the saint being in love with God, and a life of Saint Thomas Aquinas that spoke of his final vision where everything he had written seemed to him "like straw."[38]

Although I knew it had to be "like straw" in comparison with the mystical vision of God, I wanted to learn the unified worldview of Saint Thomas and see if I could come to some such view in our own times. I found a way of reading his *Summa Theologiae*, reading the body of each article but skipping the objections and replies, reading just for the integrating vision. It would take me a month to read the *Summa* in this manner, but each time I read it through I would come to a wonderful emotional tranquillity. So I found myself reading it through again and again, first when I was in college and then when I was in Rome studying theology. I was reading for thinking now or reading for vision, to experience again that sense of peaceful vision. I sought to find some modern counterpart of that unified worldview, studying Einstein's theory of relativity with its derivation of laws of nature from the thought that universal truths are true everywhere and always. But I kept coming back to Thomas's vision of everything coming from God and returning to God by way of Christ.

Still, I came to believe Saint Augustine's *City of God* was a more appropriate model of such a unified worldview in our times with our sense of history, and I set out to write my own book, *The City of the Gods*. Yet I found I had to go through a change before

I could write, I had to get in touch with my own mortality, asking myself "If I must die someday, what can I do to fulfill my desire to live?"[39] I read the Epic of Gilgamesh, the story of his quest of eternal life, and I read Heidegger's essay on death in *Being and Time*, and I found a thread going from one end of history to another. Now reading became for me a process of "passing over" into the lives and times of others, and writing a process of "coming back" to my own life and times. It was at this point that I came to my own vision of a journey with God in time. My sister, after reading my book, told me I should read Tolkien's trilogy. I found there the thoughts essential to a journey in time: "Things are meant," "There are signs," "The heart speaks," "There is a way."[40] What is more, I found again an emotional tranquillity and the sense of a peaceful vision. The journey in time, as I had first conceived it, was somewhat less peaceful, a Gilgamesh quest of eternal life, but as I settled into it, I began to feel again the peace I had known before in a vision of everything coming from God and returning to God. Eventually I thought I could see the two visions as with two eyes in focus, "The love is from God and of God and towards God."

There was still something missing, though, not just a human companion on the way but something about the way itself as a way of words. I was missing the way of music, my "road not taken"[41] in life. I had begun playing the piano when I was three years old, picking out melodies I heard on the radio, and I had begun composing when I was a teenager. So now words and music have come together for me again in this latest stage of my journey, the way of music has rejoined the way of words, and I have begun to write lyrics and set them to music. If my two visions are like two eyes, words and music are like two hands, words the right hand, for I am right-handed, and music the left. I compose music now again, but almost always to words. I am seeking some kind of unity of words and music.

A unity of words and music did exist in ancient times and was called "music" (*musike* in Greek, *musica* in Latin), as in Saint

Augustine's dialogue *On Music,* a dialogue really on the rhythms of poetry. A trace of the old unity survives in the round dance in present-day Greek folk music, where the dance has the dactylic rhythm of the ancient epics. Here I see the pattern I found also in storytelling, first an original unity, then an emergence and separation, and ultimately the prospect of a reunion. Seeking reunion, I am seeking again that emotional tranquillity I find in a unifying vision. "Seek peace, and ensue it."[42] That is my watchword. To "ensue it" is to pursue it, to follow it up. My way of ensuing it has thus been reading and writing and composing, and if "attention is the natural prayer of the soul," it has been prayer. There is an attention in reading and writing and composing that can be prayer, and that is also the source of the peace, I believe, the prayer of the soul.

I seek a unity of words and music then, like Proust, who ends with reading that turns into singing, the singing timelessness of prayer. But the unity I seek is not simply the ancient unity, "the past risen familiarly up in the midst of the present,"[43] though I do envision a singing timelessness of the heart. Something is gained in the emergence and separation that must not be lost in the reunion. That is true also in the differentiation of inner images from the real persons of a life. Something is gained in the differentiation that must not be lost in the integration, in the reunion of friend and friend. It is true also in the cycles of storytelling. Something is gained in the emergence of the human race and in the emergence of the individual that must not be lost in the reunion with humanity and with all living beings. What is gained, I believe, is "inscape," an inner landscape.

It is the inner landscape we all have within us that Proust describes in his recollections of reading, conceiving the act of reading as "that fertile miracle of a communication in solitude."[44] And it is reading that did in Don Quixote, who "so buried himself in his books that he read all night from sundown to dawn, and all day from sunup to dusk," as Cervantes tells, "until with virtually no sleep and so much reading he dried out his brain and lost his sanity."[45] Don Quixote was lost in his inner landscape. Still, it is a gain to discover the inner landscape, and it is a loss to live only in the outer landscape, so much so that Miguel de Unamuno speaks of "Our Lord Don Quixote." To live at once in the inner and the outer, I believe, is wholeness. And the way is through a reading that turns into singing, as Proust has it, through a singing timelessness of the heart. It is the reverse of what Broch's Virgil feels when insults are being hurled at him and he feels "stripped of his name, stripped of his soul, stripped of his least song, stripped of the singing timelessness of his heart."[46]

A singing timelessness of the heart is an inner time that expresses itself in song, an inner life that comes to outer expression. There is a difference between expression, the reader who begins to sing, and enactment, the reader who goes out in search of adventure. All the same, life does become an adventure when I live in the singing timelessness of my heart. It becomes the adventure of turning the truth of my life into the poetry of a journey in time. To have a name, a soul, a song goes with that singing heart, as Broch's description implies, and all seems taken away when one is heaped with insults, so much do we live in the esteem of others. Yet there is something inviolable here, "a center of stillness surrounded by silence," and I can always pass over again from silence to singing.

"The singer resumes the tale,"[47] as Albert Lord says, when I return to the poetry of my life, the sense of a journey with God in time. That sentence, "The singer resumes the tale," though Lord is speaking of epic singers, is a guiding maxim for me, coming back from an experience of loss or of disappointment, from a disruption of the journey, from an encounter with the "real" as "what does not work." When I resume the tale, the disruption becomes part of the journey, an incident on the way. I think of a friend who used to say "For a long time I was bothered by interruptions of my work. Then one day I realized the interruptions *were* my work." So it is with loss and disappointment. When I resume the tale, I tell of the experience, I sing of it. Is my journey with God in time then only the poetry of my life and not the truth? It is poetry, I want to say, but it is an expression of the truth.

To say "The singer resumes the tale" is to say "The song is far from having run its course."[48] It is like saying "The great tales never end," and that is true of the journey with God in time. When I resume the tale, I resume the journey, and the journey is far from having run its course. "The song is far from having run its course" is true also of words and music, especially if we envision the present-day differentiation of words and music giving way to an integration or a reintegration of words and music. Instead, then, of an exhausted tradition, there is the prospect of a great renewal, a reunion that will not lose "beauty," as Gerard Manley Hopkins describes it, "the virtue of inscape."[49] For myself meanwhile I see the prospect of a spiritual adventure, "a mystic road of love" on which words and music and spiritual friendship are far from having run their course.

The soul "in converse with the inscrutable"

"The converse with the inscrutable! Oh, as long as the invisible cloudy cover stretched between above and below was not pierced, the prayer brought back only its own echo; the God remained unreachable, he vouchsafed no answer."[50]

To resume the tale of a journey with God in time is to engage "in converse with the inscrutable." A friend of mine has it that prayer consists of listening to God tell us our story. I listen to God telling me the story of my journey in time. Here again "attention is the natural prayer of the soul." The attention is in the listening. Of course it seems just the opposite, I am telling the story and God is listening to me tell it. When I encounter the "real," however, as "what does not work," then indeed it does seem God is telling the story and I am involved in "an encounter with God in the real."[51] Then indeed I have to stop talking and listen. When I was talking, when I was telling the story, "the prayer brought back only its own echo." When I encounter "what does not work," however, I seem truly "in converse with the inscrutable." Just the other day I heard tell of a schoolgirl being asked "How can we make God laugh?" and her reply "By telling God our plans." Her reply is close to the adage "Man proposes, but God disposes."[52] It is the God who disposes who tells me my story. If I pay attention, if I listen then to God telling me my story, I keep reshaping and elaborating the story like an epic singer who is essentially a "listening composer."

There is a riddle song (sung by Muslim women in Herzegovina) in which a beautiful woman asks "Is there anything lovelier than I, anything swifter than a horse, anything wider than a field, anything dearer than a brother, anything deeper than the sea, anything sweeter than honey?" And a goddess (a *vila*) answers "I am lovelier than you, wider is the sky than a field, swifter is the eye than a horse, deeper is longing than the sea, dearer is one's beloved than a brother, sweeter is one's beloved than honey."[53] I like especially the line, "deeper is longing than the sea." That is the thing I seem always to be learning in prayer, that longing is deeper than I thought, deeper than the sea. Listening to God tell my story, I am always learning what is lovelier, wider, swifter, deeper, dearer, sweeter than I thought.

Once when he was a boy, a friend of mine saw a black stallion running free, and that image has always remained with him, the image of a freedom he has never attained. It is this same friend who says prayer is listening to God tell us our story. I think this image is in his mind when he speaks of God telling us our story, telling it and calling us to freedom. Anyway this image is very close to the setting of this riddle song that asks "Is there anything swifter than a horse?" It begins by describing black horses prancing beneath a green hill, "prancing, digging up the ground under them, and tugging at their golden bits." They were not running free. "They were looking at a girl by the sea, washing her white face, and rinsing her black eyes." Then the riddle begins. "Swifter is the eye than a horse," however, takes us within ourselves, and "deeper is longing than the sea" takes us deep within ourselves. It is love and longing that pierces "the cloud of unknowing" that comes between us and God, that comes between me and God, I will say, on my journey with God in time. If I can say "deeper is longing than the sea," then I know the longing that pierces the cloud of unknowing.

If I realize my longing is for God, then I can truly say it is deeper than the sea. But do I realize this? Or am I only inferring it from "our heart is restless until it rests in you"? I do feel the restlessness and it does seem like the restless movement of the sea, like the restless stamping of horses, and when I long for inward peace I long for rest in this restlessness. I long to run free on my journey with God in time, at one with myself like the black stallion my friend saw, heart-free and heart-whole in my longing and my love. Let me see if I can discern between hearing only the echo of my prayer and listening to God telling me my story, telling me mystery.

My story is mystery to me because I am in the story. I can ask like Sam "I wonder what sort of a tale we've fallen into?" But then there is Frodo's reply, "I wonder. But I don't know. And that's the way of a real tale. Take any one that you are fond of. You may know, or guess, what kind of a tale it is, happy-ending or sad-ending, but the people in it don't know. And you don't want them to."[54] What I don't know, being in it, is how my story comes out. There is something like this in the very telling of a story. It can be made to come out in different ways. "One must be aware of the tensions of association that cause the singer to go from one group of lines, or formulas, to another," Albert Lord says in *The Singer Resumes the Tale*. "The same opening may lead in several directions, and the same essential riddling core may be concluded in various ways." Lord calls this "the tension of essences."[55] When I resume the tale of a journey with God in time, I come upon these "tensions of association" or this "tension of essences" not only in the story as a whole but also in particular episodes, especially in the outcome of human relations.

I am caught in this "tension of essences" when I am caught in the uncertainty of a human relation, not knowing how it will come out, "happy-ending or sad-ending," not knowing if it will come through separation say to a happy reunion or if separation will be lasting. It is this "tension of essences," this uncertainty of outcome, that is the uncertainty principle of storytelling. The "essences," as I see them, are different kinds of relationship, such as a marriage and its story, a spiritual friendship and its story, each essence capable of carrying the whole story in a different direction.

"Tension of essences," Lord says, "is close to 'free association.'"[56] Yet I am not free to make the story come out as I will. The real freedom here is to be heart-free, as in my friend's image of a black stallion running free. I am free if I can live in the uncertainty without losing my peace. All the same, there is a kind of "free association" in my thoughts, imagining different outcomes. How am I to get through all these imaginings to peace? By listening to God telling my story. I take this to mean paying attention to what is happening in my life, paying attention especially to "the mystery of encounter," as Paul Celan calls it, to the persons who enter my life, that is, taking them as somehow belonging to my life. It means paying attention also to my own heart speaking, I believe— my own heart, for my heart may be saying something other than what I have assumed about an emotional tie. It may be my heart wants to be free of an emotional tie, wants to be free like that black stallion running free.

"Of Human Bondage, or the Powers of the Affects," Spinoza entitles the fourth part of his *Ethics*, and the fifth "Of the Power of the Intellect, or on Human Freedom."[57] Can I become heart-free simply by understanding? What Spinoza means by "intellect" or "understanding" here, I think, is a knowing that comes of loving God. To love God, he says, is simply to think of God with joy.[58] There is joy for me in the thought of my life as a journey with God in time. This is not Spinoza's way of thinking of God, to be sure, but there may be freedom for me in it, simply in thinking of the journey with God, thinking of the journey with joy. Certainly I do find peace in returning to a sense of the journey, resuming the tale, reading Tolkien for instance when emotion weighs heavily upon me.

Resuming the tale, I find, means "getting rid of what you haven't got,"[59] getting rid of the love you do not have in order to discover the love you do have. When I feel I am "not first in nobody's heart,"[60] I have to let go of that in order to find what is first in my own heart, the love of God. "Love is a joy, accompanied by the idea of an external cause," Spinoza says, and love of God is a joy accompanied by the idea of God. Others, he says, have defined love as "a will of the lover to join himself to the thing loved," but that is only a property not the essence of love. The essence is to think of the loved one with joy, and "when I say it is a property in the lover, that he wills to join himself to the thing loved," Spinoza continues, ". . . by will I understand a satisfaction in the lover on account of the presence of the thing loved, by which the lover's joy is strengthened or at least encouraged."[61] That is what I feel about the journey with God in time: my joy in the journey is strengthened or encouraged by the presence of God, who is my companion on the way.

Listening to God tell my story means being receptive to this joy, this strengthening, this encouragement. It is true, listening I am learning God is my companion and not a human being, visible and tangible. There is joy here and there is sadness. "Joy is a man's passage from a lesser to a greater perfection," Spinoza says, and

"Sadness is a man's passage from a greater to a lesser perfection."[62] The lesser here is being alone, and the greater is being unalone. My sadness is in realizing I am alone, am "not first in nobody's heart," do not have a human companion such as I have sometimes wished. My joy, on the other hand, is in realizing I am unalone and have God as my companion on the way, and especially in realizing God is first in my heart and knowing the one first in my heart is with me.

My joy is a "wandering joy," like that of Meister Eckhart, the joy of a journey with God in time. I can tell my story either way, as a story of sadness or a story of joy. As a story of sadness, it is like "a novel of obsession," a quixotic tale of loneliness and living in imagination. Listening to God tell my story, I gather, means letting go of the sadness and living in the joy of the journey with God. One who has let go, who is heart-free, according to Meister Eckhart, "experiences such a joy that no one would be able to tear it away." But such a one, being detached, "remains unsettled," he says, is ever on a journey. One who has let oneself be, and who has let God be, "lives in a wandering joy, or joy without a cause."[63] It is "without a cause" in that the joy arises out of the journey itself rather than from any particular incident on the journey. It arises out of the adventure, out of being with God on the adventure, out of running free.

Or am I to embrace both the joy and the sorrow? If "attention is the natural prayer of the soul," I have to pay attention both to the joy and the sorrow of my life, to let both joy and sorrow become prayer. Perhaps that is my way! Just as Goethe's way is to turn the truth of his life into poetry, so my way is to turn the truth of my life, joy and sorrow, into prayer. That is the true journey with God in time! If I leave out the sorrow, I am not entirely there on the journey. If I leave out the sorrow, I am not loving with all my heart and with all my soul. Perhaps then the sorrow can be caught up in the "wandering joy" of the journey, as in the words "I will turn their mourning into joy, I will comfort them, and give them gladness for sorrow."[64] Just being with God on the journey can turn sorrow to joy.

If I turn my sorrow into prayer, I give it over to God, I place my cares in God's care, and thus essentially I let go of my own sadness. I think of Hopkins and his "terrible sonnets" ("Carrion Comfort," "No Worst," "To Seem the Stranger," "I Wake and Feel," "Patience," and "My Own Heart").[65] My sadness does not compare with his, but I imagine him finding some kind of peace or relief by turning the truth of his life into poetry and into prayer. These dark sonnets seem to balance the brightness and joy of his earlier poems such as "The Windhover."[66] Maybe the joy and the sorrow of a life are in some kind of balance. Still, I don't want just to end with a balance, as in *The Woman of Andros*, "You were happy with her once: do not doubt that the conviction at the heart of your happiness was as real as the conviction at the heart of your sorrow."[67] Rather, I want to tip the balance over into the forward motion of "wandering joy."

There is indeed a balance between the conviction at the heart of my happiness and the conviction at the heart of my sorrow. The one is "as real" as the other. My happiness here, though, is joy with a cause, and the cause is the presence of the loved one. My sorrow likewise is sorrow with a cause, and the cause is the absence of the loved one. "Wandering joy," on the other hand, is "joy without a cause," a joy arising simply from the journey itself and not from any particular encounter on the journey. It doesn't balance with sorrow, therefore, but encompasses both the joy and the sorrow arising out of "the mystery of encounter."[68] For the mystery "shows itself and at the same time withdraws"[69] in my encounters.

Letting the mystery be, therefore, letting it show itself and at the same time withdraw, is the secret of wandering joy. There is a detachment here that tends to break up the sad story of obsession. Meister Eckhart speaks of letting oneself be and letting God be. I can feel especially the truth of that, letting myself be and letting God be, when I am feeling the "subjective destitution" of letting the mystery be, letting it show itself and withdraw in my life. I am always being drawn to the mysterious life I see in others, and yet I can never seem to take possession of it, can never seem "to have and to hold." I have to let it show itself to me and at the same time withdraw from me, letting me be me, letting God be God. If I can do this, if I can let it be done, I can walk with God on a journey in time. There is something elusive about God, "the inscrutable" as Broch says, and so to walk with God I have to be able to relate to this elusiveness. To me it appears in "the mystery of encounter" with other persons, as if God were showing and withdrawing in them.

I am in the mystery myself, however, I realize, being in the story and not knowing how it will come out. I live in a "tension of essences" between the story of my joy and the story of my sadness. Letting be doesn't set me above the tension of the two tales but is a way rather of relating to the tension. Prayer is my way of letting be, turning everyone and everything in the story over to God. For I find myself unable simply to let be, as in Buddhism where all these matters of "to let be"/ "to have and to hold" are so well understood, but I am able to pray, to attend to everyone and everything in my life by giving them over to God's care. I am able like Hopkins in the last of his "terrible sonnets" to "let joy sieze at God knows when to God knows what," to let life open to "unforeseen times," to let the road ahead with God open on to the prospect of "a lovely mile."[70]

> Everyman,
> I will go with thee
> and be thy guide,
> in thy most need
> to go by thy side.[71]

These are the words of Knowledge to Everyman in the old morality play where everyone and everything else turns him down except Good Deeds. But to me they are, as it were, the words of God to me on our journey in time. Although they are addressed to Everyman, they are an answer to my prayer, as if they were addressed to me. The words are before my eyes because I have been reading Hopkins in the Everyman edition and these words are quoted, as is usual in those editions, on the front page. They speak to my heart especially now that I've just reread the "terrible sonnets." Remembering the morality play, I presumed they were the words of Good Deeds, but rereading the play, I found they were the words of Knowledge. I feel moved by every clause, "I will go with thee," God will go with me, "and be thy guide," leading me by the heart, "in thy most need," in my loneliness in life and in death, "to go by thy side," God will be my companion on the way.

Knowledge is the answer here, as these are the words of Knowledge personified in the morality play, for me knowledge of the journey with God in time. It is an answer to my prayer to know God will go with me and be my guide, in my most need to go by my side. Those words "in thy most need" resonate very strongly for me, implying God is with me in my most need, in my deep loneliness.

It is true, the words of the morality play are only saying Knowledge will go with me and be my guide, in my most need to go by my side. If I take the words to be of God, I am taking Knowledge as God or God as Knowledge, God as illumining the mind and kindling the heart, thinking of God's presence as inner light . When I am in my most need, when I am feeling my deep loneliness, as I am right now, writing this, the gleam of inner light does seem to shine in my lonely darkness, "And the light shineth in darkness; and the darkness comprehended it not."[72] God is with me, but my loneliness cannot seem to comprehend this presence. Or in another version, more hopefully, "The light shines in the darkness, and the darkness has not overcome it."[73] God's presence shines in my loneliness, and my loneliness has not overcome the inner light.

So now "the singer resumes the tale," I resume the tale of the journey with God in time, and I feel the "tension of essences," not knowing how the story will come out, "happy-ending or sad-ending," but I feel the joy of the adventure itself, the joy of an adventure with God in time, a joy that cannot be taken away by the sadness of a sad ending. I remember once being inspired myself as a boy by the image of a black stallion, like my friend's image of a black stallion running free. It was in a film, and there was a haunting music that was played whenever the black stallion appeared. I couldn't remember the music exactly, but I was trying to echo it in my first composition for the piano, using chords in the whole tone scale. I remember the haunting music playing in the film for a moment even after the black stallion lost to a white stallion, as if there were a beauty and a joy that cannot be taken away by loss and sadness.

The Gate of Horn and the Gate of Ivory

"Oh, Plotia! . . . oh, if love existed, if the discrimination of love could exist in the human thicket, it would portend that together we might descend to the obliterating fountain of nothingness, to the sobering depths of the underworld, that we might descend, we sober and without illusions, going down to the primal base, not through the beautiful ivory portal of dreams which never opens for the return, but through the sober entrance of horn which would permit us to come back, retrieving in our common ascent a new fate from the last fate's embers, retrieving from the last lovelack a new love, a newly created fate, a fate in the making!"[74]

As I resume the tale, I wonder, can I retrieve "a new fate from the last fate's embers," retrieve "from the last lovelack a new love, a newly created fate, a fate in the making"? There is great hope in those words! According to Broch's tale, Virgil does in the last hours of his life make this descent to the primal nothingness and then this ascent to a new love and a new fate, although he does it without Plotia, the woman he loved in life, for the phantom of Plotia disappears from his awareness. But what new love, what new fate does he come to, if he dies at this point? A new relationship to life, I suppose, a new relationship to love and to fate. Broch's Virgil is like Tolstoy's Ivan Ilych, "In place of death there was light." If I follow Virgil back to the beginning, while facing the end, I am in effect following the path of the love that comes from God and goes to God, I am letting my own "lovelack" be caught up in the greater love.

What lovelack? There are two gates to the otherworld, according to the *Aeneid*, one of horn through which true, the other of ivory through which false dreams and visions come to us. A discerning love, "if love existed, if the discrimination of love could exist in the human thicket," would discern between image and reality in human relationships. If knowledge takes in the reality of the other, and love goes out to the reality of the other, lovelack occurs when love goes only to image and stops short of reality. If I am always falling in love with persons who are impossible dreams for me, I am not reaching them in their reality. I have to go down like Don Quixote into the Cave of Montesinos, where he learns, as in Plato's allegory of the cave, that what we take for reality is only shadow.

"I now truly understand," Don Quixote says, "that all the happiness we know, in these lives of ours, goes by like shadows and dreams, or simply withers like flowers of the field."[75] Actually I fear my own discernment between shadow and reality, between image and reality, is no more than Don Quixote's at this point, still enamored of his lady Dulcinea and not yet come to his encounter with the "real" on his deathbed. What is the "real" for me? If I think not of Lacan's "real" as "what does not work" but of Plato's "really real," then the "real" for me is the love that is "from God and of God and towards God." That, I believe, is the "real" of my longing, the "real" that comes to mind when I am feeling "deeper is longing than the sea." I think of Chesterton's chapter entitled "The Real Life of Saint Thomas" on the inner life of the saint, on his life alone with the Alone, on his feeling at the end that all he had written was "like straw." We each have a "real life," it seems, or at least the possibility of one, and I, too, have a "real life," or at least the desire for one.

A "real life" is linked with what Lacan calls "the real of desire," what I truly want in life, that for me is the Gate of Horn, and is opposed by what he calls "a way of avoiding the real of desire,"[76] and that for me is the Gate of Ivory. What is for me "the real of desire"? I believe it is to have a "real life," to be in love with God. I believe I can say with Tolstoy "God is my desire." When Max Gorky asked him what he meant by that, though, he replied "I must have wanted to say 'God is my desire to know Him. . . . No, not that.'"[77] What do I mean myself by saying "God is my desire"? What is it to have a "real life"? What is it to be in love with God? Let me see if I can discern here between the Gate of Horn and the Gate of Ivory, between the real of my desire and my way of avoiding the real of desire.

"He did not tell Gandalf, but as he was speaking a great desire to follow Bilbo flamed up in his heart—to follow Bilbo, and even perhaps to find him again," Tolkien writes of Frodo. "It was so strong that it overcame his fear: he could almost have run out there and then down the road without his hat, as Bilbo had done on a similar morning long ago."[78] That resonates with my own longing to journey with God in time, to go on an adventure with God. It is an image only but a true image, I think, this image of a journey, an adventure, coming to me through the Gate of Horn rather than the Gate of Ivory. Of that desire to go on the journey,

Tolkien says "it was so strong that it overcame his fear," and his fear he had just expressed a few lines before, "And I suppose I must go alone." That is my fear too, that I must go alone on this journey, with God, indeed, but without a human companion, visible and tangible. At times, nevertheless, my desire is like this, so strong that it overcomes my fear. What is more, it may be true for me too, as Gandalf replies to Frodo, "But I don't think you need go alone. . . ."

There is a fear of going alone and at the same time a desire to go alone with the Alone. It is the essence of personal religion, according to Festugière in *Personal Religion among the Greeks,* "to converse alone with God alone."[79] It is "the real of desire" here and expresses itself in "popular piety" and in "reflective piety" and in "the inclination to retirement." But because of the fear of going alone, we find "a way of avoiding the real of desire," of not going on. All the same, "I don't think you need go alone. Not if you know of anyone you can trust, and who would be willing to go by your side—and that you would be willing to take into unknown perils."[80]

There is a thicket here of contrary desires and fears, to go alone and unalone, but "the road goes ever on and on . . . until it joins some larger way where many paths and errands meet."[81] This going on and on, this joining a larger way where many ways meet, speaks to my fear of death and of aloneness. For the journey is essentially "alone with the Alone" but it is also unalone in the joining of many paths. Even though I feel my life has been like Don Quixote's, my journey like Don Quixote's sallies into the world, I have been living in reality too as the road goes on for me. And when "the singer resumes the tale," as I do now, and I know I am living in my imagination, and I fear it is too late for anything else, still I see I am getting somewhere as the road "joins some larger way where many paths and errands meet," for me words and music and spiritual friendship.

"Real presences,"[82] as George Steiner calls them, I find in words and music and spiritual friendship. In my life words and music create relationships with others, and spiritual friendship is the relationship they create. Again, "real presences" are what I find in going alone with the Alone, the presence of God, and even in simply going alone, my presence to myself. So in spite of all my loneliness, I am not really alone. Nonetheless I feel the deep loneliness and longing that I believe is part of our human condition, the condition at any rate of the emerged and separated individual. Perhaps then the answer to loneliness is to become aware of "real presences." Perhaps the answer is in the growing awareness of "real presences" that comes about on "the road of the union of love with God."

If I can locate the path of love that comes from God and goes to God, then indeed I have found the "larger way where many paths and errands meet." I imagine the path of love to be like "the path of the sun" as it is called or "the road of the sun," the apparent way the sun moves through the constellations in its rising and setting in the course of the year. The love that comes from God and goes to God has an apparent path or way as it passes through the "real presences" of a life. Each human relationship in a life is like a constellation and the divine love is like the sun rising in that constellation as the relation becomes important in the life and passing on to another as the focus of life changes. "Attention is the natural prayer of the soul," and the focus of my attention does shift, but it is particularly on "the mystery of encounter," and it moves as the mystery seems to be moving, from one presence to another in my life, and my attention, the natural prayer of my soul, follows along its apparent path, though sometimes it lingers where the mystery has withdrawn and does not follow on to where the mystery is showing.

I keep saying "seems to move" and "apparent path" with the thought that all this is relational, is about my attention following the showing and withdrawing of mystery in the relationships of my life. I don't mean to say that it is not real, that it comes through the Gate of Ivory rather than the Gate of Horn. It is like walking along the shore and seeing the sun making an apparent path of light on the water, coming to you and following you as you walk. The sun is real, and the light is real, and it does really come to you, and yet others walking in the opposite direction will see the sunlight coming along a path to them and following them too as they walk. So the path of divine love is the same and not the same to one and to another.

Passing over to the path of divine love in other people's lives leads into "popular piety," and coming back with new insight to the path of divine love in my own life leads into "reflective piety."[83] My fear of going alone can keep me from coming back, my fear of losing the togetherness I find in "popular piety." When I come back to myself, nevertheless, it is with a longing for solitude, "the inclination to retirement," as Festugière calls it, to "retirement for solitary prayer" as in the Harmony of the Gospels. There has to be a balance between solitude and the human circle, I can see, between the "reflective piety" of solitude and the "popular piety" of the human circle, as I turn the truth of my life into the words and music of prayer, if "the road goes ever on and on . . . until it joins some larger way where many paths and errands meet." For "the road goes ever on and on" in the "reflective piety" of solitude, and "it joins some larger way where many paths and errands meet" in the "popular piety" of the human circle.

I feel very vulnerable in coming back from the human circle to solitude. It is the loneliness that makes me vulnerable. It is the loneliness: a divided heart, a wandering eye, a stifled cry. My heart is divided between solitude and the human circle, my eye wandering from one person to another, from one thing to another, a stifled cry my prayer. It is by uttering my cry in prayer that my heart becomes whole and my eye full of light. It is by uttering my stifled cry that I turn the truth of my life into the words and music of prayer. So my "real life" is my life of prayer, the attention I give to the "real presences" in my life and that I express in words and music.

What is my stifled cry? I ask myself. It is the cry of love, I believe, that comes from God and goes to God. Why is it stifled? Ultimately, I believe, it is because the love is unknown, because we love with a love we do not know. It is by turning the truth of my life into the words and music of prayer that I utter love's cry, that I come to know the love. I think of the experience A. J. Arberry describes of translating the Koran. Although he was not translating his own feelings into words, his own feelings were resonating as he translated the words from Arabic to English, and he called the result, keeping to Islamic ideas about translation, not *The Koran* but *The Koran Interpreted*.[84] I imagine the peace he was feeling to be like the peace of prayer, to be like the peace I feel when I translate the emotions I feel in a time of loss or disappointment into the words and music of prayer. And I think of the peace as an experience of the love of God, and I think of prayer as the cry of love unstifled. Prayer is the unstifled cry of the heart.

Although I speak of God in the Koran and of God in Spinoza's *Ethics*, it is "God with us" that resonates with my heart. "Behold, a virgin shall be with child, and shall bring forth a son, and they shall call his name Emmanuel, which being interpreted is, God with us."[85] It is "God with us" I am speaking of when I speak of a journey with God in time. What attracts me to the Koran and to the *Ethics* is the sense of the presence of God. I am finding in the Koran interpreted, if I may borrow Arberry's term, and in the *Ethics* interpreted, the God who is found in those moments of "retirement for solitary prayer" in the Harmony of the Gospels, the God of Jesus, the God who is with us on our journey in time.

If the cry of the heart is for "real presences" and at bottom for the presence of God, it is felt especially in moments of loneliness and of "subjective destitution." When I have lost a human presence that I thought essential to my life, I find there are other human presences, though no one of them replaces the one I have lost. These other presences, though many, can be as one to me, however, as if God were loving me through them and I were loving God in them. I find myself recording in my diary each loving encounter with another, noting how someone called or I met someone or someone sent a letter, and I find myself concluding "It is God who loves me" and "It is God I love." The absence of one friend is not replaced by the presence of other friends, and yet there is the presence of One in the many. It may be my sorrow and my longing for lost human presence that is speaking, but if I let the cry of my heart become prayer, then indeed I am in the presence of God, and I can exclaim in prayer "It is you who love me! It is you I love!"

How can I tell if this prayer comes through the Gate of Horn or if it comes through the Gate of Ivory? By peace of heart. If I can find peace in this prayer, then it expresses the true cry of the heart. No doubt, I can be so attached to someone or something that I become like Tolkien's Gollum, "unable to find peace or relief ever in life again."[86] Or it can be that letting be and openness to the mystery comes for me only with repeated and continuous prayer. What makes the prayer true is the letting be and openness to the mystery. On the other hand, that is what the prayer does, enable me to let be and be open where I could not. It enables me to find peace and relief by enacting the letting be, giving over all I have lost to God, by enacting also the openness to mystery, letting God be present where I have been experiencing only loss and absence.

Say "Friend" and enter,[87] the password in Tolkien's story, is also the password here in passing through the Gate of Horn. By letting be and being open to the mystery of the divine presence showing itself and withdrawing in the presences of my life, I am a friend even to a lost friend, letting the friend be and being open to the mystery in our friendship. Letting be, Heidegger says,[88] means turning towards, not turning away, and though he is speaking of letting things be, what he says seems true also of letting persons be. There is a detachment in love and in friendship, without which one would become "unable to find peace or relief ever in life again" when loss occurs. Sometimes you find you have put something behind you, even though you had set your heart on it, put it behind you without making the conscious effort to do so. That can happen also with friendship. You find you have let it go, even though you are still a friend to your friend. You have put the expectations of friendship behind you while letting it be and being open to its mystery.

If I say "Friend" and enter, I find myself on a journey with God that includes human friendship. There is a willingness to walk alone, I mean, not a will to walk alone, and so there is an openness to "the mystery of encounter." "Friend" is the password because it is the experience of friendship with its letting be and openness to mystery that enables me to understand friendship with God. It is the nature of the journey with God in time that "you may find friends upon your way when you least look for it" and "it would be well to trust rather to their friendship than to great wisdom."[89]

My prayer then, "It is you who love me! It is you I love!" if it is not to be a denial of human friendship, has to be balanced by something like the prayer Kathleen Norris records in *Dakota*, "Keep me friendly to myself, keep me gentle in disappointment."[90] When I meet with disappointment in human friendship, I am tempted, like Aesop's fox who could not reach the grapes, to say "They were probably sour grapes anyway." I am tempted to say human friendship is not really what I wanted anyway but divine friendship. "Keep me friendly to myself" goes with "It is you who love me," and "keep me gentle in disappointment" goes with "It is you I love." It is true, divine friendship is really what I want. It is "the real of my desire," but I find I want divine friendship in human friendship. So when I meet with disappointment in human friendship, I find myself praying "Keep me friendly . . . keep me gentle . . . ," and I find in divine friendship that friendliness, that gentleness.

God is inclusive, therefore, and the love of God is inclusive, and to be alone with the Alone is to be all one with the All One. That is probably the meaning of the famous phrase *monos pros monon* in the *Enneads* of Plotinus, not so much "alone with the Alone" as "one with the One."[91] If my life is a journey in time and God is my companion on the way, then I may find friends on my way when I least look for it—that is not surprising if God is my companion—and it would be well to trust rather to their friendship than to myself alone.

"Love is the reality"

"And although he himself hardly knew what it meant, a phrase presented itself: 'Love is the reality.' So it became audible and suddenly it was no longer enigmatic. For the gods blessed man with love to ease the pang of his lusts, and he who has partaken of this blessing perceives reality; he is no longer a mere lodger in the realm of personal consciousness in which he is caught. And again he heard: 'Love is the reality.'"[92]

When I have partaken of this blessing, that of love and friendship, I am "no longer a mere lodger in the realm of personal consciousness" but am able to perceive reality that is greater than myself. I am able to perceive reality not simply as what frustrates the imagination of my heart, Lacan's "real" as "what does not work," but as something larger than myself in which I can be caught up, Plato's "really real." We perceive reality, according to Plato in *The Republic*, when we come to the vision of the Good. I see something like Plato's vision of the Good in the vision of the love that comes from God and goes to God, "The love is from God and of God and towards God." It is the experience of human love and friendship, I believe, that enables us to perceive the reality of the love of God. If I experience only the pang of my lusts, I am trapped in the realm of personal consciousness and am unable to see beyond myself. That is the danger in a time of loss, when I experience the loss of love and friendship: I can become trapped once more in myself. Even in a time of loss, nevertheless, I can remember love, and so I can come to the vision of the love of God, my vision of the Good, and I can set out, as I have been doing here, on the mystic road of love. It becomes essential, then, in a time of loss or of disappointment to move in the direction of love, to become caught up in the vision of the Good and in the love of God rather than be left behind in the realm of subjective destitution.

There are three stages here: first, that of ignorance, where I know only the pangs of lust and am trapped in my own subjectivity; second, that of the experience of human love and friendship, where I know the blessing of love and how it eases the pangs of lust; and third, that of perception of reality, the vision of the Good, when my experience of human love and friendship enables me to perceive the reality of divine love. The insight into divine love comes for me with the sense of life as a journey in time, but it depends on "the mystery of encounter" with human love and friendship on my way. So it is the combination of the sense of a journey and the experience of human love that leads into the vision of a love that comes from God and goes to God.

If the love of God consists of thinking of God with joy, as Spinoza says, then it is the love of God that sustains me in a time of loss when I am in danger of relapsing into the subjectivity of destitution with its pangs of lust. I do indeed find sustenance in the sense of being on a journey in time, reading Tolkien, for instance, to reinforce my own vision, and feeling the presence of God in his sense that things are meant, there are signs, the heart speaks, there is a way. The vision of the Good, therefore, if I am on the right track here, is not a vision of God pure and simple, face to face, not a vision of God abstracted from life and from time, so much as a vision of life and time in terms of God, a vision of the love that comes from God and goes to God, the love that passes through life and time. It is a knowledge of love. It is a sense of the journey with God in time. And so the joy that is the love is a joy in "God with us" (for Spinoza too it is a joy in God as the substance of our lives), a rejoicing in the presence of God. The vision of the Good, therefore, is not a vision of something abstract, as in Aristotle's critique of Plato, but is a sense of presence.

As the light of the world "the Good may be said to be not only the author of knowledge to all things known, but of their being and essence," Plato has Socrates say in *The Republic*, "and yet the Good is not essence, but far exceeds essence in dignity and power." And he has Glaucon respond "with a ludicrous earnestness," as if to underline the hyperbole, "By the light of heaven, how amazing!"[93] It is more than essence. It is the essence of an essence that far exceeds essence in dignity and in power, or, if I read *ousia* as "presence" rather than "essence,"[94] it is more than presence. It is the presence of a presence that far exceeds presence in dignity and in power. Let us see what it would mean to say all this of love, to see the love of God as setting us free from the pangs of subjective destitution.

Love is light in the darkness of my heart, that is how it sets me free from the pangs of subjective destitution. Freud's famous question "What do women want?" can be turned around into a personal question "What do I want?" There is a darkness in my heart that does not know what it wants. And if I pray with Saint Augustine "our heart is restless until it rests in you" or write in my diary like Tolstoy "God is my desire," still I find there is a gap between the question and the answer. How to close the gap? How to bring the light of love to shine in the darkness of my heart? It is true, taking love of God on its simplest terms as joy in the thought of God, for me joy in the thought of being on a journey with God in time, I find the love of God does indeed shine in the darkness of my heart, but as I said before, quoting John, "the darkness comprehended it not." My heart with its pangs, with its destitution, does not comprehend the love. That is the gap, the incomprehension of my heart. Is there an insight now, a spark of light, that will leap over this gap?

Human love and friendship is able "to ease the pang" of our "lusts," according to Broch, and one "who has partaken of this blessing perceives reality," is "no longer a mere lodger in the realm of personal consciousness." Is this, then, the insight, the standpoint of human love and friendship? It does not take away the standpoint of "personal consciousness," but it does give me another place to stand, and I am no longer trapped in my own subjectivity. It comes between divine love and the darkness of my heart, thus it comes in the gap, even in a time of loss, when I am most feeling the gap. It comes there in other loves and friendships and in the memory of lost love and friendship, and my heart is able to comprehend human love and friendship even when it cannot yet comprehend the divine.

"You could not endure even the Absolute Good itself for ever, if it bored you,"[95] Aristotle says in his discussion of friendship in the *Nicomachean Ethics.* It can bore you when you are feeling the darkness of your heart, for boredom is a craving for excitement, a craving that doesn't know what it wants. And boredom can come about when the Absolute Good is being thought of as something abstract or separated from us. When I think of God, rather, as my companion on a journey in time, I am not so easily bored, for I am living always in "the mystery of encounter." And the joy itself I feel that is the love of God, my joy in the thought of God, is a joy arising out of my perception of life as a journey in time where "you may find friends upon your way when you least look for it," where your hope is always leading into the unhoped-for.

What then do I want? When Freud asked "What do women want?" he was thinking of something specific to the feminine soul.

"The great question that has never been answered and which I have not been able to answer, despite my thirty years of research into the feminine soul," he said to Marie Bonaparte, "is 'What does a woman want?'" (*Was will das Weib?*).[96] The question I am asking is at once more personal and more universal, "What do I want?" If I take the most subjective and destitute standpoint, the answer is in "the pangs of lust." If I take the more encompassing standpoint of human love and friendship, the answer is in the "I and thou." And if I take the most comprehensive standpoint, that of the larger reality in which I am caught up, the answer is in the love of God.

There is a choice here, to live in one standpoint or another. The very existence of the more comprehensive standpoints means I am not trapped in that of subjective destitution. If I choose then to go on with the journey with God in time, I am choosing to live in the most comprehensive standpoint. I am choosing like Frodo in Tolkien's story to go on alone, only to find that I am not alone after all. Frodo decides to go on alone and take no friend with him into danger, but he finds to his relief that he cannot escape his friend Sam, and so he goes on with Sam into the unknown. "It is no good trying to escape you. But I'm glad, Sam. I cannot tell you how glad," he says. "Come along! It is plain that we were meant to go together."[97] I can choose thus to live in the more comprehensive standpoint of the love of God, but it is the very nature of the larger standpoint to include the less comprehensive one of human love and friendship.

Unfortunately, it is also its nature to include the least comprehensive standpoint, the narrow standpoint of subjective destitution and its pangs. Thus in Tolkien's story there comes a point of crisis when Frodo falls under the spell of the Ring of Power ("I do not choose now to do what I came to do. I will not do this deed. The Ring is mine!")[98] and then afterwards, even though he escaped, being saved from himself by Gollum, there are moments when he is troubled by the memory of the fear and the darkness. In those dark times he clutches a white gem given him by the Lady Arwen. "When the memory of the fear and the darkness troubles you," she said, "this will bring you aid."[99] He wears the gem on a chain around his neck just where he wore the lost ring. I need some kind of talisman like that, I can see, to remind me of the love of God and the journey with God when I am feeling the pangs of subjective destitution.

"It is gone forever, and now all is dark and empty,"[100] Frodo says, lying on his bed in one of those moments of subjective destitution. That is the feeling one has also in a time of loss, when one is feeling the loss of a human love and friendship. It is also the feeling one has at the end of psychoanalysis, according to Lacan, when one has lost all one's illusions. "But the fit passed," and so it is in a time of loss, the fit passes. It is a help in those moments to remember human love and friendship, the love and the friendship one does have, and it is a help to remember the love of God. It is not a matter of sustaining one's illusions so much as sustaining one's sense of a larger reality and not becoming trapped in oneself.

If I look for a talisman to remind me of the love of God, I think of a Muslim friend in Istanbul who used always to be fingering his prayer beads. When we parted, he gave me his beads, and I still have them, a precious gift, thirty-three beads in three groups of eleven to correspond, when told three times, to the ninety-nine names of God. Telling the beads is a method of "remembering God" (*dikhr Allah*), just as telling the rosary beads is a method of remembering God and the Mother and the Child. I had a rosary but I didn't offer it to my Muslim friend. I suppose I wanted to let the gift be a gift rather than an exchange. I could not help stealing a glance, though, at my friend's hands, after he had given me the beads, to see if they were twitching nervously, but his hands were quiet and I was all the more impressed, realizing he really had been remembering God.

My own way of remembering God is prayer too, following that maxim of Malebranche, "attention is the natural prayer of the soul," attention to the persons and the situations I am meeting on the journey in time with the thought that time is "a changing image of eternity," a changing image rather than sheer repetition. For I find that a changing image is able to hold my attention more than a round of repetition, corresponding as it does to the restless movement of desire that goes constantly from one image to another. The repetition of the divine names seems to correspond, rather, to the repose of the heart in God. And so if "our heart is restless until it rests in you," my way of remembering God corresponds to the restlessness of the heart while my friend's way corresponds to the rest, and I have yet to learn how to come to rest in God as he does. The divine names for me are still abstract, but for him they are real, like my sense of God being with me on the journey, guarding and guiding me. Perhaps the truth is simply that I am on a journey with God and not yet at rest in God.

There is a timeless place in our hearts, and perhaps there somehow we can come to rest in God. "We have found by experience that unconscious mental processes are in themselves 'timeless,'" Freud says in *Beyond the Pleasure Principle*. "That is to say to begin with: they are not arranged chronologically, time alters nothing in them, nor can the idea of time be applied to them."[101] Perhaps my journey with God in time is headed toward repose in God in timelessness, and the divine names that I can understand now only in terms of "God with us" in time I will be able to understand in terms of us with God in timeless repose. I see an image of this in Tolkien's story at the end, Bilbo and Frodo sailing into the West.

"If your hurts grieve you still and the memory of your burden is heavy, then you may pass into the West, until all your wounds and weariness are healed."[102] There is a link here between timelessness and healing. Instead of time healing it is timelessness that heals. There is healing, nevertheless, in the sense of a journey with God in time, for it is a sense of timelessness in time, and there is repose there too, a rest in restlessness. I can see the seeking of rest and healing in "the inclination to retirement" that Festugière finds in personal religion. If "love is the reality," however, I expect "retirement into oneself"[103] brings healing and rest when it means retirement into the timeless place in our hearts. Love belongs to our "unconscious mental processes," as Freud calls them, insofar as we love with a love we do not know. By dwelling in the timeless place in our hearts, by following "the inclination to retirement," we come to know the love and are able to speak out of unconscious mental processes that have become conscious and say, like the old Bedouin to Lawrence of Arabia, "The love is from God and of God and towards God."

When "unconscious mental processes" become conscious, however, they enter into time, and the love of God too, when it becomes conscious, enters into time. My own sense of a journey with God in time seems to embody just that, a conscious awareness of the love of God and with it a conscious awareness of time. Still, my sense of time as "a changing image of eternity" is a sense of timelessness in time, and so it has a connection as yet with the unconscious mental processes from which it has arisen. What is more, the timelessness has become itself a conscious experience, as in Hammarskjold's saying, "We all have within us a center of stillness surrounded by silence," and so my journey in time can be seen as heading toward a repose of heart in conscious timelessness.

When Freud speaks of "unconscious mental processes" as "timeless," he probably has in mind something like the "Once upon a time" of fairy tales, or the time of wish-fulfilment in dreams, "In the old times, when it was still of some use to wish for the thing one wanted." Conscious processes are in the time of *memento mori*, the time of conscious mortality and the realization that we will die. Love is able to survive the passage to consciousness, to exist not just in the world of dreams and fairy tales but also in the world of time and mortality. "Love is the reality," therefore, in a very comprehensive sense. It is the reality that is common to the world of dreams and the world of mortal existence. In passing from the one world to the other, however, one can experience a loss in love. "She said that she heard your heart calling out to her sometimes and she began to understand how she gave you something to love, and then took it away again,"[104] Patricia McKillip says in a story, describing such a loss.

If I awaken to the world of mortal existence from living in my imagination, like Don Quixote on his deathbed, I begin to understand how I was given something to love and then it was taken away. I begin to understand, that is, how "The love is from God and of God and towards God." Surviving the passage to consciousness, my love is still there, but when its object is taken away it becomes love pure and simple. It feels like loss at first, but then it begins to feel like something in its own right, something joyful, a joy in the journey of life, a joy in the thought of being with God on the journey, in the thought of "God with us." I am coming to know the love of God. George MacDonald calls this "proving the unseen."[105]

When I run into something that thwarts me, when I run up against the "real" as "what does not work," then I am ready for the "really real," I am ready for "proving the unseen." When I am thwarted, I am tempted to lose confidence in myself, to lose confidence in God. Letting go of the thing I set my heart upon, I am able to come to myself, I am able to come to God again and the love of God and the joy of the journey with God in time. For as long as my heart is still set upon the thing that was given and taken away it seems everything I do is useless, even prayer seems useless. When I let go of my heart's desire, or what I thought was my heart's desire, I come to understand my heart. Feeling the peace of letting be and being open to the mystery, I realize my heart's desire is not what I thought. It is like the moment in a screenplay by Andrei Tarkovsky when the Russian icon painter Andrei Rublev meets Theophanes, his dead master. "Didn't you go to heaven?" Andrei asks him. "What difference does it make?" Theophanes answers. "All I can say is that it's all quite different from what you all imagine. I must go."[106]

"Proving the unseen," I am coming to know love, I am coming to know it is all quite different from what I imagined when I was living in my imagination. My heart is calling out and I begin to understand it, how I was given something to love and then it was taken away again, and now I find peace in letting be and being open to the mystery. My love is "without a cause" like my joy, without a visible and tangible human cause, that is. It comes from the unseen and it goes to the unseen. It comes from God and it goes to God. "Proving the unseen," I try to give it expression in prayer, I try to find the words and the music of heart's desire.

"It was the word beyond speech"

"A floating sea, a floating fire, sea-heavy, sea-light, notwithstanding it was still the word: he could not hold fast to it and he might not hold fast to it; incomprehensible and unutterable for him: it was the word beyond speech."[107]

If I try to name my heart's desire, it eludes me when I think of the losses and disappointments of life, and yet I find peace in letting be and being open to the mystery that "shows itself and at the same time withdraws," that gives me something to love and then takes it away again. Although I cannot "hold fast to it," as Broch says of "the word," its showing and withdrawing somehow gives me hope. What hope? "The essence of being is itself releasement"[108] or "letting be," and there is peace for me in that, but I still have hope, for being open to the mystery leads me upon an adventure. My heart's desire is "a floating sea, a floating fire, sea-heavy, sea-light." Its name is "the word beyond speech." What word? For

Heidegger it is "Being," as in the sentence of his poem, "We are too late for the gods and too early for Being." For me it is the "I am" of the Gospels, translated "It is I" or "I am he" and expressing the Shekinah, the presence of God.[109] It is the Word that was in the beginning, according to the Gospel of John, and that is in the end, according to *The Death of Virgil.* I hope it will be that for me, as Virgil on his deathbed comes to "it was the word beyond speech" I will come to "In the end is the Word."[110] For to die that way is to complete the circle of love that comes from God and goes to God. It is to let go of everyone and everything and find everyone and everything again in the "joy of man's desiring."[111]

Such a hope, to complete the circle of love, is an eternal hope, a hope of eternal life, for the circle of love goes ever on and on. Say I have a dream in which I embrace a friend I have not seen or even thought of in a long time. I see this very sweet embrace as an image of completing the circle of love. It is an image of my hope. Should I take it more literally as a wish-fulfilment in dream of my desire to embrace this friend in real life? It may be that too, but its deepest resonance in me is with a longing to close the circle of love. Taking it this way, I am interpreting it *a lo divino*, like the mystics, using love songs to express the love of God. Like a love song, my embrace in a dream can look to wish-fulfillment with strong sexual overtones and yet at the same time, like a mystical song, it can convey a deep yearning to realize the love of God in my life.

To complete the circle of love is to bring back to God the love that comes from God, to complete the circuit or the circulation of the love, like the veins carrying the blood back to the heart, where it will be renewed and flow again through the arteries to all parts of the body. Here the vision is of everyone and everything coming from God and returning to God, or of the love of God coming to everyone and everything and returning again to God. "In the beginning was the Word" is the expression of the love coming through the arteries, and "In the end is the Word" is the expression of the love returning through the veins. As I contemplate this vision, I feel like Black Elk saying of his life, "Now that I can see it all as from a lonely hilltop, I know it was the story of a mighty vision given to a man too weak to use it."[112] This vision I am contemplating, the love coming from God and returning to God like blood flowing through the arteries and back through the veins to the heart, is "a mighty vision." And I am "a man too weak to use it." Or is there a way I can use it?

To use a vision is to realize it. For instance, for Black Elk to use his vision of two roads, a red one, "the road of good," and a black one, "a fearful road, a road of troubles and war,"[113] would have been to walk the red road of good himself and to lead others on it, to lead his people on it. To use my vision of love coming from God and going to God would be to walk the mystic road of love myself, what I am trying to learn here, and to lead others on it, what I am doing by writing all this down. I am learning to walk and to talk here, to walk the mystic road of love and to talk to others about it. If my love of God is essentially joy in the thought of God and of a journey with God in time, I am learning to walk in "wandering joy."

Along the pathway all things speak, Heidegger says. "In what remains unsaid in their speech—as Eckhart the old master of letter and life says—there is God, only God."[114] To walk in "wandering joy," I gather, is to listen to all things speak but it is to listen above all to "what remains unsaid in their speech." It is to listen to "the word beyond speech." I see a connection between this and Polanyi's saying "we can know more than we can tell." We too speak, and in what remains unsaid in our speech there is God, only God. When I say "Things are meant" and "There are signs" and "The heart speaks" and "There is a way," I am not mentioning God, and yet God is there in what I am saying. My learning to walk and talk here is learning to walk along the way and to listen to the heart speak and to discern the signs and to decipher the meaning of things, and it is learning to speak myself with an awareness that what remains unsaid in the speech of things and signs along the way as well as in the speech of the heart there is God, only God.

I am learning to walk and to talk, not like a baby first learning but like a person recovering from a stroke, learning again, recovering from the losses and disappointments of life."Everything speaks abandonment unto the same (*Verzicht in das Selbe*)," Heidegger concludes. "Abandonment does not take. Abandonment gives. It gives the inexhaustible power of the Simple."[115] That is what I am learning, learning again. "Is the soul speaking?" he asks. "Is the world speaking? Is God speaking?"

It is the soul that is speaking of "abandonment," of "not taking," of "giving," for these are acts of the soul. What is meant by "abandonment" here is "letting be." In Heidegger's thinking "letting be" is a relation to things, letting things be, and is at once a Yes and a No to them, letting them into our lives and at the same time leaving them outside. He is thinking of technology, and "the meaning pervading technology hides itself,"[116] he says, and that is what he means when he speaks of "mystery" and how it "shows itself and at the same time withdraws." If I apply the idea of letting things be to human relations, as in those words "she heard your heart calling out to her sometimes and she began to understand how she gave you something to love, and then took it away again," I am speaking of letting be with respect to "something to love," and the showing is in the giving and the withdrawing is in the taking away. My own giving then is in giving back what has been taken away and not taking what is no longer given. Still my heart is calling out.

It is the world that is speaking of "the same," for it is the world that exhibits "the eternal recurrence of the same events," as Nietzsche called it, though not perhaps in the way Nietzsche understood it. There are recurring patterns in the story of a life, and I can see the recurring pattern of finding and losing in my own life. "I lost, and then I found, and then I lost again," I can say as in William Morris's story *The Well at the World's End*. "Maybe I shall find the lost once more." And maybe I can appropriate the answer given there, "The lost which was verily thine shalt thou find again."[117] If I am on the right track here, however, I will recover by "abandonment unto the same," by letting go of "the lost," by letting be and being open to the mystery of finding and losing and finding once more.

It is God who is speaking of "the Simple," I want to say, for it is God, I believe, who wields "the inexhaustible power of the Simple." If I look more closely at the mystery of finding and losing, I can see in it the paradox of the Gospels, "One who finds one's soul will lose it, and one who loses one's soul for my sake will find it."[118] It is as if the soul, or God and the soul, were the mystery that "shows itself and at the same time withdraws." It is because of "the Simple." "The Simple seems monotonous to the distracted. The monotonous brings weariness. The annoyed find only the uniform. The Simple has fled. Its quiet power is exhausted."[119] That is the mystery withdrawing. It is when I discover again "the inexhaustible power of the Simple" that the mystery shows itself again. Perhaps that is the key to finding the lost once more. It is "one who loses one's soul for my sake" who "will find it." That phrase "for my sake" seems to say that if I let go for "God with us," if I let go of everyone and everything for the sake of the journey with God in time, I will find everyone and everything again in time with God on the journey.

God and the soul, that is the question, according to Saint Augustine in his *Soliloquies*, "May I know me, may I know thee," and that is the answer for me, to know me, to know thee, to live in an "I and thou" with God. That is "the Simple" for me, and there I find "the inexhaustible power of the Simple." For there in "retirement for solitary prayer" the turning wheel of the world is grounded for me on the road of life, and so the vehicle moves forward as the wheel turns. I move forward instead of being trapped in the perpetual recurrence of the same events. And that is what it means for me to be on a journey with God in time. It means to be free from or free of or free towards the perpetual repetition of the same events.

Considering the recurring patterns in the story of a life, Freud says in *Beyond the Pleasure Principle*, "we may venture to make the assumption that there really exists in psychic life a repetition-compulsion, which goes beyond the pleasure-principle."[120] He ascribes repetition thus to the soul rather than to the world. It is "beyond the pleasure principle" because often it brings pain rather than pleasure, like the recurring pattern of finding and losing I find in my own life. That pain is what makes me want to ascribe it to the world rather than the soul. If I ascribe it to the soul, then I am saying there is something in me that wants not only to find but also to lose the "something to love" I have found. If I ascribe it to the world, then I am saying the repetition comes of that "something to love" that is always being given to me and then taken away. It is true, my loving that "something to love" is the work of the soul. So the recurring pattern is due both to the soul and to the world, both to my loving and to the nature of the thing I love. If I am always coming to love something that is impossible for me to have and to hold, then I am always getting myself into a situation of inevitable loss.

"Being and having," as Marcel says, that is my choice here. To be free of the perpetual repetition of the same events of finding and losing I have to turn from having to being, from "I and it" where "it" is that "something to love" to "I and thou." I have to turn to the "I and thou" of the journey with God in time and let that be the basis for an "I and thou" of spiritual friendship. "Every means is an obstacle," Buber says in *I and Thou*. "Only when every means has collapsed does the meeting come about."[121]

Seeing the "I and thou" as a relation of person to person rather than an experience of having and holding, Buber is able to say things like this, "Every means is an obstacle"—that is, an "it"—and "Only when every means has collapsed does the meeting come about," only when the "it" has been taken away does the "I and thou" shine forth. The loss is of the "it," not of the "I and thou." "I thought I lost you,"[122] one of Patricia McKillip's characters says, only to discover the "thou" is still there, the relation has endured. So it may be also for me. And when I turn from having to being, from "I and it" to "I and thou," I may find that is all that matters, the "I and thou" has endured the loss of "it," has endured, gone through, and survived, and has shone forth and does shine forth as "I and thou." "Only when every means has collapsed does the meeting come about." That has been true for me before and will, I trust, be true again.

So the repetition does go on, "I lost, and then I found, and then I lost again. Maybe I shall find the lost once more." I become free towards the repetition of finding and losing, though—if not free from it—by turning from having to being, from "I and it" to "I and thou." Is the "I and thou," then, my heart's desire? If it is, why am I so obsessed with the "I and it"? These are both "primary words"[123] according to Buber. What of "the word beyond speech"? That is the word of heart's desire. I can't seem to settle for "I and thou," and yet I can't seem to be happy with "I and it." It is somehow the wholeness of "I and it" and "I and thou" that is the heart's desire. "The word beyond speech" is gift, not theft like "I and it" nor exchange like "I and thou." It is pure gift, and that is what my heart desires.

If I turn from having to being, nevertheless, I am still open to having. It is like Solomon's dream where God says "Ask what I shall give you" and Solomon says "an understanding mind"[124] and God is so pleased that he gives Solomon not only an understanding mind but everything else besides, all the things he wanted and did not ask. It is as if God were telling me too, "Ask what I shall give you," and I too were learning now to say "an understanding mind" or perhaps better, as in another translation, "an understanding heart" or "a heart to understand."[125] I am learning from finding and losing and finding again and losing again to ask for an understanding heart, to understand why I find and lose, why I am given something to love and it is taken away again, the why of "I and it" in order to enter fully into "I and thou" without despairing thereby of "I and it." It is true, "I and it" becomes theft if I hold on after it has been taken away. It can be gift, though, after I have let it go, and it is exchange, the communion of "I and thou," that gives me freedom to let go.

Is there communion, is there exchange in "I and thou" when "I and it" has been taken away? Yes, the giving and the giving back of "it," of "something to love," is the exchange. It happens only when I am willing to give back what has been taken away. As long as I am unwilling there is only loss. "A heart to understand" here is a willing heart. My willingness is to give and give back, my hope is to receive. As I meditate on Buber's words and my own experience of relation, I can see I am heading toward a pure "I and thou." Still, I can see there is a balance between "I and thou" and "I and it." There is a balance between relation and experience. "As experience, the world belongs to the primary word *I-it*," Buber says. "The primary word *I-thou* establishes the world of relation."[126]

I can experience the relation itself, being conscious of standing in relation to God and to myself and to others, but that is compatible with an absence as well as with a presence of the other, and when the other is absent it is pure relation that I experience. Is that enough for me? Is it enough to sustain the relation in the absence of the other? The "I and thou" with God is especially that, pure relation and an experience of pure relation. "The Lord can be like a lot of nothing" a friend said to me once, a friend who was very given to prayer. Still, every experience I do have can be illumined by the relation with God, as is suggested in those sentences "Things are meant" and "There are signs" and "The heart speaks" and "There is a way." And so the journey with God in time can seem very rich in experience. Taken this way it can sustain me in the loss or the absence of friends where the pure relation can seem indeed "a lot of nothing."

What then is the presence of God? Is it pure relation? Is it an experience of pure relation? Certainly for Buber it is pure "I and thou," and he calls the Gospel of John "the Gospel of pure relation."[127] But there is an "it" in the Gospel of John, the "one" in "I and the Father are one,"[128] and this "one," I believe, names the heart's desire, the oneness of "I and thou." I desire the "I and thou," but is it not the oneness that I desire, the union, the reunion? "Absence is to love as wind to fire," it has been said, "it blows small love out but makes great love blaze."[129] So is absence to the heart's desire. It blows other desires out, desires for this and that, but it makes heart's desire blaze, for heart's desire is God's own love in us.

So Buber is right, the Gospel of John is truly "the Gospel of pure relation," and pure relation is what the heart desires or, I want to say also, the experience of pure relation. If "I and the Father are one," the "one" is "I and the Father." So if I desire the "one," it is the "I and thou" that I desire. Saying this, I find myself back at my starting point, "Once upon a time of loss I set out on a mystic road of love." That is how I began, but now I see the "I and thou" was never lost. Was the "it" lost? "The necklace was never lost," a Swami said, beginning to speak of "getting rid of what you haven't got."[130] He was telling the story of a woman who thought she lost her necklace but came to realize she had it all along. That is like realizing, as the Swami also said, "God dwells in you as you." If I see the relation with God as Buber does, as "I and thou," I am more vulnerable to loss. I can lose the "it," that "something to love," and yet, as I am learning, the "I and thou" can survive.

I am heading toward pure relation, therefore, toward a pure "I and thou," but pure relation is also an experience, as I am conceiving it, and so there is a balance of "I and thou" and "one." "I and thou are one," I can say, paraphrasing "I and the Father are one." There is something liberating about this. It liberates me from pining over loss. What is more, it means my life story need be no longer "a novel of obsession." I am ready now to walk "the mystic road of love," as I have been calling it, I am ready for "the way above."

The Way Above

"Subtle is the Lord God, but not malicious,"[1] Einstein said. One obsession can cast out another, I find; a preoccupation with an idea can cast out a preoccupation with a feeling. It is as if the engrossing idea were truly a godsend, something sent by God to free you from the engrossing feeling. When it has proven to be limited, then, one idea among other ideas, it leaves you free and open again to mystery, able again to pray with attention, to be attentive to persons and situations as signs, as having a meaning, to listen again to your heart speaking, to find again the way.

All the same, the way for me past a fascinating idea, for instance an idea connecting time with space and matter, is an idea charged with feeling, an idea connecting time with life and death. My fascination is always with time, it seems, the mystery of time "a changing image of eternity." Is there a way from time to eternity, a rainbow bridge you can cross during life or maybe only in death or maybe in life as well as in death? There is a translation by Shelley, I just found, of Plato's *Symposium* where love is that rainbow bridge. "The divine nature cannot immediately communicate with what is human," Shelley translates, "but all that intercourse and converse which is conceded by the Gods to men, both whilst they sleep and when they wake, subsists through the intervention of Love."² Love here is Eros, the heart's longing, and so the heart's longing, according to this, is the rainbow reaching from time to eternity.

There is also love that is Philia, friendship, and love that is Agape, divine love. I think of the conversation at the end of the Gospel of John about human and divine love, "Do you love me?" and "Yes, Lord, you know that I love you," where these two words for love are being used, as if to say "Do you love me with the love that is of God?" (*agapas me*) and "Yes, Lord, I am your friend" (*philo se*). That dialogue of Jesus and Peter continues until Jesus goes from "Do you love me?" (*agapas me*) to "Are you my friend?" (*phileis me*) and Peter, very upset, answers "Lord, you know everything, you know I am your friend" (*philo se*).³ I gather that their friendship, according to this, can lead into the love that is of God, and that this divine love is what Jesus is calling Peter into when he concludes, "Follow me" and tells how Peter will come finally to lay down his life for his friend. So there is the Platonic ascent of Eros from passion for the individual to ecstasy in contemplation of the ideal, but then there is the movement from longing through friendship to love that is of God. The Way Above, for me therefore, leads from Eros through Philia to Agape, from heart's longing through spiritual friendship to the love of God. And there is, like Diotima for Socrates or Beatrice for Dante, a guide, for me Sophia, the figure of Holy Wisdom. I call her Ayasofya, as Hagia Sophia is called in Istanbul.

All these Greek names for love, Eros and Philia and Agape, as well as for wisdom, Hagia Sophia and its derivative Ayasofya, name for me the Way Above. I see here an ascent of love, like the one Socrates says he learned from Diotima, an ascent that includes his from passion to contemplation, that comes like his to "a life spent in contemplation of the beautiful" and goes on then to a sharing of that life in spiritual friendship and to a sense of being moved in all this by the love that is "from God and of God and towards

God." I see an ascent, that is, in which the longing becomes the love. Let me see now if I can walk here in the steps of love.

Ayasofya: Wisdom as Guide

"Such a life as this, my dear Socrates," exclaimed the stranger Prophetess, "spent in contemplation of the beautiful, is the life for men to live; which if you chance ever to experience, you will esteem far beyond gold and rich garments, and even those lovely persons whom you and many others now gaze on with astonishment, and are prepared neither to eat nor drink so that you may behold and live for ever with these objects of your love!"[4]

I come to an impasse on the path of pure feeling, unable to get around the experience of lack and loss, and on the path of pure thought, unable to realize my thoughts on time as "a changing image of eternity." So I turn in the direction of thought charged with feeling, time in relation to life and death. "Thoughts without content are empty," Kant says, and "intuitions without concepts are blind."[5] My intuitions without concepts on the path of pure feeling are indeed blind. "I lost, and then I found, and then I lost again. Maybe I shall find the lost once more." I don't know what to expect until I bring concepts to bear upon my intuitions. My thoughts without content, on the other hand, on the path of pure thought are indeed empty. I have to bring them into relation with matters of life and death where I have feelings that run deep enough to give them content. "Nature hides her secret because of her essential loftiness, but not by means of a ruse,"[6] Einstein says, explaining what he means by "Subtle is the Lord . . . ." I have to connect with feelings deep enough to match that "essential loftiness" if I am to understand "a changing image of eternity." There is no "ruse" for me to unravel just by means of pure thought.

Wisdom is in the union of thought and feeling, it seems; it is a knowing that comes of loving. Diotima seems to embody for

Socrates such a union, such a knowing, and Beatrice seems to embody it for Dante, and Ayasofya embodies it for me. Was Diotima a real person? Was Beatrice alive for Dante after her death? Is Ayasofya real and alive for me? The experience of being in the place called Ayasofya or Hagia Sophia was very real for me, an experience of encompassing peace.[7] That was my meeting with her, and my relation with her, the "I and thou," is real for me.

If I bring before Wisdom the lack and loss I experience, I see it "under the aspect of eternity," and I realize in this very matter the thought of time as "a changing image of eternity." I see loss as of "I and it," and I see "I and thou" as the eternal in our relationships. What is more, I see the connection between this and my relationship with the figure of Wisdom herself, as if I had been seeking in my lack and loss what I find in Ayasofya herself, "for in her there is a spirit that is intelligent, holy, unique, manifold, subtle, mobile, clear, unpolluted, distinct, invulnerable, loving the good, keen, irresistible, beneficent, humane, steadfast, sure, free from anxiety, all-powerful, overseeing all, and penetrating all spirits that are intelligent and pure and most subtle."[8] These, according to the Wisdom of Solomon, are the twenty-one attributes of Sophia, the figure of Wisdom.

There is a poem called "Three Meetings," by Vladimir Solovyov, describing his three encounters with the figure of Holy Wisdom, though he never calls her by name. "Eternal friend" he calls her and says "I shall not name you."[9] I wrote a song myself, inspired by his, as part of a song cycle called "Ayasofya":[10]

> I met you
> dwelling in a human heart;
> I found and lost you,
> and I lost and found
> my soul in the lost hills;
> and we shall meet again

as child and child,
and heart shall speak peace
unto heart.
A human face
and your face in the azure light,
a human soul
and your soul of a universe,
and we shall meet again,
face to face,
and heart shall speak peace
unto heart.
To let friend befriend
and soul besoul,
to let be
and be heart-free
and heart-whole,
and we shall meet again
as friend and friend,
and heart shall speak peace
unto heart.

I can see now, reading the words of my song again, that there is an ambiguity. I was having difficulty differentiating between Ayasofya and her human embodiments. That is my task now, I can see, to differentiate. "Sometimes I read in your eyes a sorrow too deep to express, a long lonely road that flickers through your being at the moment of our parting," a friend wrote to me. "Sometimes I think you aren't really even seeing me at that moment, but that you are communing for a second with someone else."

It is clear to me that Ayasofya, not only with those twenty-one attributes of Spirit but even as I have experienced her myself, as *an encompassing peace*, is a divine, a transcendent figure. All the same, her light is not like the harsh light of the sun at noonday but like the soft light of the moon or of a lamp lit at night, and so it is easy to see her in a human being whose light is soft and comforting. I remember what a young Turkish woman said to me, seeing me spend hours every day in the place called Ayasofya, walking and praying, sitting and writing, "You are in love with Ayasofya!"[11] I think of the words ascribed to Solomon in the Wisdom of Solomon, "I loved her and sought her from my youth, and I desired to take her for my bride, and I became enamoured of her beauty."[12] Bold words! Yet maybe that is it! I have simply to realize I am in love with Ayasofya! To be in love with her is to love wisdom, but it is to pass from an "I and it" with wisdom to an "I and thou."

What would an "I and thou" relation be like with the figure of Wisdom? I think of a children's story, *At the Back of the North Wind* by George MacDonald. I suppose I am thinking you must become a child to enter the kingdom of God, and so you must become a child to enter into an "I and thou" with Holy Wisdom. Anyway the story is of a child who is befriended by the North Wind, a feminine spirit that "blows where it wills, and you hear the sound of it, but you do not know whence it comes or whither it goes."[13] One night, according to the story therefore, the North Wind comes into the hayloft where the child sleeps, and that is the beginning of many adventures for him until at last he reaches the country at the back of the North Wind "whence it comes" and "whither it goes."

"I want you to take me to the country at the back of the north wind,"[14] the child says to her. "You see," she answers, "it is very difficult for me to get you to the back of the north wind, for that country lies in the very north itself, and of course I cannot blow northwards,"[15] and yet "It is easy enough for me. I have only to consent to be nobody, and there I am. I draw into myself, and I am on the doorstep."[16] There on the doorstep she is very still and unresponsive. "You don't care for me anymore," the child says, almost crying. "Yes, I do," she answers. "Only I can't show it. All my love is down at the bottom of my heart. But I feel it bubbling there." "What do you want me to do, dear North Wind," he says. "What do you want to do yourself?" she replies. "I want to go into the country at your back," he says. "Then you must go through me . . . you must walk on as if I were an open door, and go right through me."[17]

"It was when he reached North Wind's heart," McDonald says, "that he fainted and fell. But as he fell, he rolled over the threshold, and it was thus" the child "got to the back of the north wind."[18] So there is paradox in an "I and thou" relation with a figure such as that of Wisdom. If I think of her as the Spirit who blows where she wills, then I hear the sound of her but don't know whence she comes or whither she goes. To go there I must become nobody, as she does, I must go through her, walk on as if she were an open door and go right through her. It is when I reach her heart that I faint and fall and roll over the threshold. For her love for me is down at the bottom of her heart, and I must go through her heart to get to the bottom of love and discover the "from and of and toward" of love.

This image of passing through the heart of Wisdom makes me think of the Heart Sutra in Buddhism which is described as "the heart of perfect wisdom." The difference is between the "I and thou" with Wisdom I am seeking here and what the Heart Sutra describes as an "I and it," or rather, if we take into account the Buddhist doctrine of "no-self" (*anatta*), a "no-I and it" with wisdom. That "no-self" of Buddhism is like the "nobody" in Mac-Donald's story. Speaking of the country "at the back of the north wind," the North Wind says "that is my home, though I never get farther than the outer door. I sit on the doorstep and hear the voices inside. I am nobody there." She adds "you will be very glad some day to be nobody yourself. But you can't understand that now."[19] That "nobody" I will venture to say is the same as the "no-self," and the relation of "no-I and it" may be the other side of "I and thou." Anyway, the Heart Sutra is about the *emptiness* of "I and it." It is very short and begins with the words "Homage to the Perfection of Wisdom, the Lovely, the Holy!" and it ends with the words "Gone, gone, gone beyond, gone altogether beyond, O what an awakening, all-hail!"[20] As I read it, the Heart Sutra is saying that wisdom is in going, going, going beyond, going altogether beyond the "I and it," that this is true awakening. And as I read MacDonald's story, becoming "nobody"—that is, going beyond the "I and it"—is how to get to the back of the North Wind. But there at the back of the North Wind "heart speaks to heart."

All this I seem to be learning from lack and loss: loss is of "I and it," but "I and thou" is eternal, even the "I and thou" of one human being and another, and one human heart speaks to another, and the learning here, the learning from lack and loss, is an "I and thou" with Holy Wisdom herself, and her heart speaks to my heart.

I am "learning from suffering,"[21] as Aeschylus says, but coming not to an "I and it" with suffering so much as to an "I and thou" with Wisdom. I see the Buddhist insight into suffering as dissolving the "I and it," just as love itself dissolves it, according to Broch, "and he who has partaken of this blessing perceives reality: he is no longer a mere lodger in the realm of personal consciousness in which he is caught." I see the Christian insight, on the other hand, as coming to the "I and thou." There are only a few sayings of Jesus about Wisdom, one that "Wisdom is justified by all her children" or "by her deeds" in answer to the criticism that Jesus is "a glutton and a drunkard, a friend of tax collectors and sinners."[22] The other is his own criticism of his generation, "the Wisdom of God said I will send them prophets and apostles, some of whom they will kill and persecute."[23] That is in Luke. In Matthew it is Jesus himself who says "I will send you prophets and wise men and scribes, some of whom you will kill and crucify . . ."[24] as if to imply he himself is the Wisdom of God, as Paul afterwards says, "Christ the power of

God and the wisdom of God."[25] As always with Jesus, "I and thou" goes over into "I am."

"But when he said 'I am' he was not saying '*I* am,' pointing to himself, I think," my friend David Daube said to me, "but 'I am,' pointing to the divine presence, to the Shekinah, the presence of God in him and through him."[26] And here again, the Shekinah is a feminine figure. Maybe we can say the Shekinah, the divine presence, and my Ayasofya, the divine wisdom, are one and the same.

My own relation with her is "I and thou" not "I am," though I too must go right through her like the child passing through the heart of North Wind—"you must go through me . . . you must walk on as if I were an open door, and go right through me." And to do that I must become "nobody" like her, letting go of the "it" that makes me somebody, "I and it," somebody in relation to something. But it seems I never become utterly transparent like Christ but at best translucent. The "I am" comes out of utter transparency, it seems, and Ayasofya herself is transparent like North Wind in the story. The child "stared at her in terror, for he saw that her form and face were growing, not small, but transparent, like something dissolving, not in water, but in light," MacDonald tells. "He could see the side of the blue cave through her very heart. And she melted away till all that was left was a pale face, like the moon in the morning, with two great lucid eyes in it."[27] That is what this transparency is, a dissolving in light, and that is what "I am" conveys.

It is all I can do, however, to pass from the opaque "I and it" to the translucent "I and thou." My relation with Ayasofya is at best one of translucence where I am able to pass on her light to others, but that is short of the transparent "I am." Still, just to pass on the light instead of obstructing it, that is a noble task. "He was not the light," John says of John, "but came to bear witness to the light."[28] If "beauty," as Hopkins says, is "the virtue of inscape,"[29] then this translucence is the beauty, the virtue of my inscape.

Nevertheless there is something in me that does not dissolve in light. It is real, at any rate, if nothing else. But if Ayasofya dissolves in light, like North Wind in the story, is she real? That is the question the child asks North Wind toward the end of the story. "Please, dear North Wind, I am so happy that I'm afraid it's a dream," he says. "How am I to know that it's not a dream?" At first she answers "I'm either not a dream, or there's something better that's not a dream." "But it's not something better—it's you I want, North Wind," he persists. Then, after they had been sitting silent for a while she says, "I think that if I were only a dream, you would not be able to love me so." "I see! I see!" the child exclaims. "How could I be able to love you as I do if you weren't there at all?"[30] I think I see too, for while knowledge takes things in, love goes out to things. Knowledge takes in the reality of the other, as much as it can, but love goes out to the other in the other's reality, and so love can go beyond knowledge. We can love someone even though we don't fully understand them. And so it is love that proves the reality of the other. Here again it is a matter of "proving the unseen" and it is love that proves it.

But what of that element in me that does not dissolve in light? I think here of alchemy, of transforming base metal into gold, and of Jung's symbolic interpretation of alchemy, of transforming the base metal of one's life into the gold of wisdom. There is a four-stage process going from the Nigredo, the dark of life, to the Albedo, the light or brightness of life, to the Rubedo, the redness or fullness of life, to the Citrino, the gold of wisdom. And it is Ayasofya who can lead me through this process, for her light is not blinding, as the brightness or the gold of the sun, but is soft and comforting and counseling, and "Things are earth-possible in her light and can be lived."[31] I have, then, with her aid to pass from the dark of my life, my sense of lack and loss, to the brightness, getting rid of the love I haven't got to find the love I have, to the redness, giving myself heart and soul to the love I have, to the gold, living clear down in my heart.

My first step, from the darkness to the brightness of my life, is the one I have been taking from the opaque "I and it" to the translucent "I and thou," by letting go of "it," the something I am holding on to that makes me somebody. "I have only to consent to be nobody," as North Wind says in the story, "and there I am."[32] Notice in her words "I have only to consent" and "there I am." So even though she consents to be nobody she is still someone. Even if I let go of "it" and become "no self," as in Buddhism, no "I and it" really, there is still "I and thou." In fact, that is when "I and thou" shines forth, when I let go of "it" and cease to be "I" in relation to "it," when I cease to be "I and it." The darkness of my life then is "I and it," and the brightness of my life is "I and thou," and when I am content with "I and thou," when I am content to live purely in an "I and thou" relation with my friends, lost and found, then I am living in the light, then I am living in an "I and thou" with Ayasofya herself.

As I go on, though, considering these steps, letting go of "it" and living in the "I and thou" and on to the further steps of being heart and soul in the "I and thou" and living clear down in my heart, I have an uneasy feeling that this is like alchemy in another way — it never quite works. There is a better way, and that is suggested in the Wisdom of Solomon in the long prayer for wisdom, "give me the wisdom that sits by thy throne. . . ."[33] Or, better still, in the direct address to Holy Wisdom in the antiphon that goes with this prayer of Solomon in the Liturgy of the Hours,

> Wisdom of God,
> be with me,
> always at work in me.[34]

It is a better way because this invocation of Wisdom goes right into the "I and thou" with Wisdom, is already an exercise of "I and thou." It is better because it goes into the "I and thou" by way of prayer and lets that dissolve the "I and it," instead of trying to let go of the "it" and come thereby into the "I and thou." I find it much easier to pray than to let go, although praying can be a letting go, turning everything over to God.[35] In this invocation of Holy Wisdom I am seeking to dissolve the "it" but by grace rather than works, by Wisdom being with me and working in me. Still, the very invocation of Wisdom accomplishes the thing I am seeking, the "I and thou" with her. I pray this prayer every day, and I imagine Ayasofya answering in words like those of Saint Teresa:

> No fear,
> no false hope,
> no untoward desire,
> no sadness
> settle in your heart
> to take away your peace,
> for all is passing,
> only One unchanging,
> —waiting
> comes to all fulfillment,
> holding to the One
> you will lack nothing,
> One alone
> enough for you.

This song from "The Green Child" is my paraphrase of Saint Teresa's "Nada te turbe, nada te espante . . ."[36] The *nada* here is "no it" or "no I and it." So I appeal to Ayasofya, and my appeal to her is already an "I and thou" with her, and she answers, and her answer is comfort and counsel, comforting me for the inevitable loss of "it" and counseling me to live in the eternal "I and thou." She can lead me then through these alchemical stages, and first from darkness to brightness in the ascent of Eros or longing, "for she knows and understands all things," as is said in the Wisdom of Solomon, "and she will guide me wisely in my actions and guard me with her glory."[37] Her guiding and her guarding I need because there are pitfalls, I can see, especially on the path of love as longing, because we love with a love we do not know, I believe, a love we do not understand, because we are in love with God without knowing it.

Eros: Love as Longing

"If I knew what you ask, O Diotima, I should not have so much wondered at your wisdom, nor have sought you out for the purpose of deriving improvements from your instructions."—"I will tell you," she replied: "Love is the desire of generation in the beautiful, both with relation to the body and the soul. . . . Generation is something eternal and immortal in mortality. It necessarily, from what has been confessed, follows, that we must desire immortality together with what is good, since Love is the desire that good be forever present to us. Of necessity Love must also be the desire of immortality. . . . Love is a tendency towards eternity."[38]

If time is "a changing image of eternity," and desire is the restless movement from image to image, then desire is of eternity, though desire is always taking itself to be of the image. "Love is a tendency towards eternity," as Plato has Diotima say to Socrates. It is when I see things under the aspect of eternity that I realize this, and that is usually in prayer. When I pray for what I want, my wanting is changed, my desiring appears under the aspect of eternity, and I pass from the image to the reality. It is not that I get what I want when I pray, but my wanting changes in the light of eternity, and what I thought I wanted gives way to what I really want. I thought I wanted someone or something, but when I bring that into the light of eternity I realize "all is passing, only One unchanging. . . . One alone enough for you." So prayer is my way, letting my longing become prayer, letting it carry me on the ascent of love.

Seeing things under the aspect of eternity is possible apart from prayer, it is true, as when Spinoza or Wittgenstein speak of "the aspect of eternity." With Spinoza this is a matter of seeing things in terms of God; with Wittgenstein it is a matter of seeing things in terms of the universe as a whole. "To view the world *sub specie aeterni* is to view it as a whole," Wittgenstein says, " a limited whole."[39] Spinoza too speaks of "the face of the whole universe which, although it varies in infinite ways, nevertheless remains always the same."[40] Taking prayer as I have been taking it, "attention is the natural prayer of the soul," I can see these kinds of seeing as prayer or as turning into prayer when seeing becomes attention, somewhat as when hearing becomes listening.

"Feeling the world as a limited whole—it is this that is the mystical," Wittgenstein says, and "It is not *how* things are in the world that is the mystical, but *that* it exists."[41] It is the wonder you experience when you contemplate the stars in the night sky. It is what happens for me in prayer: I come to feel the world as a limited whole, I pass from what I think I want, having to do with how things are, to what I really want, having to do with existence, that I am, that you are to whom I pray. I feel very close here to Meister Eckhart and his basic conviction that "Existence is God" (*Esse est Deus*),[42] for to say it is "the mystical" is close to saying it is "the eternal" as well as to saying it is "the divine." Longing comes to rest, it seems, as it passes from "how things are in the world," which "varies in infinite ways," to "that it exists," which "remains always the same." I pass in prayer from the changing to the unchanging face of the universe.

It is true, I am conceiving this changing and unchanging face of the universe as "thou" rather than "it." Time, which "varies in infinite ways," is "a changing image of eternity," which "remains always the same." Or time is like a half-face, like the half-face of a little girl with cancer on the other half of her face, as Flannery O'Connor suggests, a face that is "grotesque but full of promise,"

promise of the full face that is eternity. Let us see if longing, when it becomes prayer, can carry us into a face-to-face, a half-face to full face.

"Most of us have learned to be dispassionate about evil, to look it in the face and find, as often as not, our own grinning reflections with which we do not argue, but good is another matter," Flannery says. "Few have stared at that long enough to accept the fact that its face too is grotesque, that in us the good is something under construction." She is thinking here of Teilhard's vision of the universe as something under construction and on its way toward Omega. The face of the universe is like the face of Mary Ann, the little girl whose face was half devastated by cancer. "When we look into the face of good," Flannery says, "we are liable to see a face like Mary Ann's, full of promise."[43] As she sees it, the promise is of Omega, the full face, the eternal face we are always glimpsing in the changing image that time is. Like Saint Anthony at the end of Flaubert's *Temptation of Saint Anthony*, seeing the face of Christ in the rising sun after his night of trial and temptation, we see the full face only after we have looked into the grotesque half-face of good.

Seeing the universe as "the divine milieu," Teilhard sees the good under construction in a twofold process of "divinization of our activities" and "divinization of our passivities."[44] It is especially this latter process that Flannery sees in the grotesque half-face of Mary Ann, quoting Teilhard's phrase "passive diminishments." "The story was as unfinished as the child's face. Both seemed to have been left, like creation on the seventh day, to be finished by others," she says of the memoir of Mary Ann written by the sisters who took care of her. "The reader would have to make something of the story as Mary Ann had made something of her face."[45] I see a universal truth in this. Our story too is as unfinished as the child's face; it seems to have been left, like creation on the seventh day to be finished by others. We have to make something of our story as

Mary Ann made something of her face. Making something of our story, as I understand it, is telling our story in such a way as to draw meaning from it and direction into the unknown ahead of us.

"Our gaze is turned to the stream of time—or rather to that small stretch of its flow by which we sit and which we call the present," Ivar Ekeland says, meditating on the painting *The Temptation of Saint Anthony* by Hieronymus Bosch, where you can see the saint sitting by the stream, wrapt in contemplation, while all the monsters of dread and fascination come up behind him to frighten or seduce him. "But the hermit is lost in contemplation. His mind has touched the land of eternal truth. His assailants feel that he is out of reach, and their efforts become perfunctory," Ekeland observes. "He does not see the two-legged tower which squats at his side, wielding a mallet, or the menacing creatures which approach behind his tree. The arrow aimed at him will miss, and the devil's claw will not reach him. All above him the sky spans blue."[46]

If we can imagine Saint Anthony, as in Flaubert's ending, gazing on the face of Christ in the rising sun, we can see why he is lost in contemplation. It is the hope he sees there of eternal life. Love is "the desire of immortality," as Diotima says to Socrates, "a tendency towards eternity." It is with eyes of faith in Christ risen from the dead that the saint gazes on the rising sun as if it were the rising Christ. Flaubert spends that whole long account describing the temptation itself, the dread and fascination that would take away the saint's hope, cause him to lose his faith, divert his love toward another object. Only Flaubert's next to last sentence, printed in small letters in the French editions, stage directions as it were, tells of the object of his contemplation, "Right in the middle, and on the disc itself of the sun, shines the face of Jesus Christ."[47]

There is something here for us in this sense of vision, an eye that can contemplate the face in the rising sun. Flannery speaks of "our gain in sensibility and our loss in vision," as she meditates on the face of Mary Ann, our gain in sensibility to the suffering of a child like Mary Ann and our loss in vision, in the ability to see in her face the face of the universe. "If other ages felt less, they saw more," she says, "even though they saw with the blind, prophetical, unsentimental eye of acceptance, which is to say, of faith."[48] When we do see with the eye of vision in our own age, it seems, we come to see something like Teilhard's vision of Omega, or like Flannery's vision of the full face promised in the half-face, or like Solovyov's vision of the one I call Ayasofya, when he saw her at sunrise in the desert and saw all things in her as if she were the soul of the universe. I find myself trying to combine vision and sensibility in her soft light.

Sensibility and vision, this is my aim in the reunion of words and music I am trying to achieve in my song and dance cycles. If "it is not *how* things are in the world that is the mystical, but *that* it exists," then sensibility and vision are in the wonder of existence. There is sensibility in my "Once upon a time of loss," and there is vision in "I set out on a mystic road of love." It is in the wonder of existence that sensibility and vision come together, that lack and loss and love come together, for it is in that wonder that I am able to let be and be open to the mystery. If "it is not *how* things are in the world that is the mystical," I am able to let be in lack and loss, and if the mystical is "*that* it exists," I am able to find "a mystic road of love."

What can you do, though, with the simple wonder of existence, "*that* it exists"? I find myself getting trapped again and again in "*how* things are in the world," both in my sensibility, getting caught up in lack and loss, and in my vision, getting caught up in trying to work out a theory of time as "a changing image of eternity." As I write this I am listening to Messiaen's *Quartet for the End of Time*, and that gives me the hint of an answer, that eternity is in contemplating the wonder of existence, that time comes to an end in contemplation. "But the hermit is lost in contemplation. His mind has touched the land of eternal truth. . . . All above him, the sky spans blue." This music of Messiaen reveals the mystic road of love. "It may be what we cannot know we should not speak of, but sing of it we may,"[49] Wilfrid Mellers says of Messiaen's music. To sing of it, that is what I am seeking in a reunion of words and music. Or instead of "speak of" and "sing of" I should say "speak to" and "sing to," for I want to enter into an "I and thou" with the soul of the universe.

When I speak of "the soul of the universe," I am speaking in metaphor of the divine presence in the universe. I don't mean to say the universe is literally animated by a soul. The soul of the universe is a matter of poetry, I mean, not metaphysics, and yet real for all that, as the divine presence is a real presence. Mathematics is said to be "poetry of the universe," and that is the poetry I want to use to realize time as "a changing image of eternity." I want to connect the changing image with the relativity of time and with insight into image.[50] But I can see now why visions of time seem inadequate when time itself is the horizon of thought, whether time is being related to life and death or to space and matter. I can see why Saint Augustine's meditation on time in his *Confessions* seems to have greater depth. It is because it is carried out in the presence of eternity.

If I meditate on time in the presence of eternity, I have a kind of Archimedean point of reference outside of time. It is like and unlike the beginning of time, "the big bang" in present-day cosmologies. "The big bang is not a point of space-time," Robert Osserman says in *Poetry of the Universe*, "but a reference point outside providing the zero point of time, just as 'absolute zero' (zero on the Kelvin scale) does not correspond to an attainable temperature in the real world, but a point off the scale to which all other temperatures are referred."[51] Eternity, though, is more than "the zero point of time." "If we take eternity to mean not infinite temporal duration but timelessness," Wittgenstein says, "then eternal life belongs to those who live in the present."[52] I want rather to say *eternal life belongs to those who live in the presence.* Eternity is the divine presence. "What if this present were the world's last night?"[53] Donne begins a Holy Sonnet. The beginning and the end, the present and the presence, all come together in vision, but sensibility comes with presence, presence in the beginning and in the end, presence in the present.

Eternal life belongs to those who live in the presence. That is my answer. That is the fulfillment of love as longing, of love as a tendency toward eternity. It comes after the equivalent of Saint Anthony's temptation in a life. Bosch's *Temptation of Saint Anthony*, the one at Madrid, I mean, like Flaubert's meditation on Breughel's, seems to end in living in the presence. That is the serenity where dread and fascination dissolve, the rest where the restless heart comes to repose, the real meaning of eternity always being revealed in the changing image, the screenplay of time.

Meditating on time in the presence, like Saint Augustine at the end of his *Confessions,* I come to the kind of peace he comes to, not so much an end as a beginning, like the very beginning of time. And so he goes on to meditate on the beginning. What becomes then of time's relation to life and death? And what of time's relation to space and matter? If time is a changing image, like a screenplay, it seems to embody the restless movement of imagination from image to image, expressing the restless desire of the heart. For Augustine the Reader,[54] as he has been recently called, time is like the sequence of words or syllables, like those of a hymn such as "Deus Creator Omnium," his favorite hymn, composed by Saint Ambrose. A changing image, like a screenplay, is itself an image of seeing. A sequence of words and music is an image of hearing. Reading, as he learned from Ambrose, can also be silent, and time is silent.

Time is silent, but if I mark time in the presence of eternity, I come to a "music of spheres." For if I view time as "a changing image of eternity," using mathematics as my poetry, I can view the universe from the "event horizon,"[55] the sphere that circumscribes for us the limits of visibility. Thus I divide the universe in two: one hemisphere is the visible world we know and the other is what lies beyond our event horizon, beyond the limits of observation. My universe, then, is like Dante's double sphere, one earth-centered and the other God-centered, or like Riemann's hypersphere or spherical space that figures in Einstein's General Relativity. One hemisphere of such a universe is the realm of time as we know it, and the other, if not of eternity, is of time beyond the event horizon.

It becomes an "undivided universe," though, if I view it in the pervasive presence of eternity. "The shape of the Dante-Riemann universe is what mathematicians call *spherical space* or a *hypersphere*,"[56] Osserman says in *Poetry of the Universe*, and in such a space, as in an infinite sphere, the center is everywhere and the circumference is nowhere. The center everywhere I take to be the presence of eternity. Thus it is when Beatrice leads Dante to the event horizon of his world, he sees something in her eyes he had not seen or thought of before, and when he turns to follow her gaze he perceives a point of intensest light with concentric circles wheeling around it. He sees the vision of God. But he is amazed, for he has been rising to ever widening circles, from the earth to the widest circle of all, the "event horizon" as we call it, the Primum Mobile as he calls it. And yet now, looking into Beatrice's eyes and looking directly for himself, he perceives circles converging on a luminous center. What is more amazing still, it is as if the center is everywhere and the circumference is nowhere.[57]

Eternity then, if I think of eternity as a pervasive presence, is an infinite sphere whose center is everywhere and whose circumference is nowhere.[58] So for me too, "the music of the spheres" or "the harmony of the spheres" really exists, but it is in the relation of time to eternity, its relation to life and death, and its relation to space and matter. You hear the music of the spheres when heart speaks to heart, as Beatrice speaks to Dante, and you see the harmony, if I can speak here of "seeing," when you look into the eyes of another, as Dante sees the vision of God in the eyes of Beatrice. Seeing God, I gather, is like going from hearing to seeing, from hearing the music of the heart to seeing the harmony of the universe.

It is an illuminating experience, I find, to read Dante and Riemann side by side, to read the Cantos of Dante's *Paradiso* side by side with Riemann's Inaugural Lecture. Space, according to Riemann, is "finite but unbounded,"[59] and so the center is everywhere, the circumference nowhere, or as Beatrice says to Dante,

> I've seen the whence of every where and when.

Or so I translate "io l'ho visto dove s'appunta ogni *ubi* ed ogni *quando*."[60] She is speaking of that point of intensest light, and I am taking her to mean the luminous center, though we don't see it, is everywhere and always. I can imagine traveling all the way to the event horizon like Dante and looking so far into the past as to see the beginning of time, a point of intensest light, "the whence of every where and when," but "feeling the world as a limited whole—it is this that is the mystical," feeling it as finite but unbounded, brings me back again to the present and makes me aware of presence here and now, the presence in where and when I am.

Why is it hard to stay in the presence? Why does my mind wander? "Most of the problems in performing twentieth-century music," it has been said, "are related to rhythm."[61] Rhythm is the difficulty also in living in the presence. There is a rhythm of time in relation to life and death, a rhythm of time in relation to space and matter, and a rhythm of time in relation to eternity. The secret of keeping time is to discern the presence in the present. Like Dante seeing the point of light in the eyes of Beatrice, I find I can see the presence in human eyes, when they are eyes of knowledge and love. Discerning the eternal presence in human eyes is my way to vision.

Philia: Love as Friendship

"It came about, as I believe by your providence through your hidden ways, that she and I were standing leaning out of a window overlooking a garden . . . after the exhaustion of a long journey, we were recovering our strength. . . . Alone with each other, we talked very intimately. . . . We asked what quality of life the eternal life of the saints will have. . . . And while we talked and panted after it, we touched it in some small degree by a moment of total concentration of the heart. And we sighed and left behind us 'the firstfruits of the Spirit' bound to that higher world, as we returned to the noise of our human speech where a sentence has both a beginning and an ending."[62]

These words of Augustine in his *Confessions* describe the experience he shared at Ostia with Monica, his mother, just before her death. Here, after his conversion to faith, they are no longer son and mother so much as friend and friend, sharing their deepest longing and their highest vision. It is as though every human relationship reaches its climax in friendship, and the essence of spiritual friendship is in sharing the deepest longing of the heart and the highest vision of the mind. I think again of something my friend Helen Luke said to me in conversation a couple of years before she died, "I believe friendship is the highest thing." I think she meant the highest of all human relationships, and that seems to agree with the idea I am coming to here, that every human relationship reaches its high point when it turns into friendship. It is a way to vision because vision is shared in friendship along with the heart's longing.

Coming back "to the noise of our human speech where a sentence has both a beginning and an ending," Augustine and Monica are coming back to time from having "touched" eternal life "in some small degree by a moment of total concentration of the heart." If our principle is right, *eternal life belongs to those who live in the presence*, their touching of eternal life is a concentrated moment of living in the presence. And then their coming back to time is a coming back to the storytelling that occurs in ordinary conversation where the story and each sentence in the story has a beginning and an ending. It is a coming back to life that starts with birth and ends with death, and yet the sense they have of eternal life means it is not life that begins and ends so much as the life story.

I can see Augustine's *Confessions* as prolonging such intense moments of living in the presence and sharing them with others, as he originally shared with Monica, by casting the whole story into the form of prayer. Going one step further, as he seems to suggest by his repeated references to Ambrose's hymn "Deus Creator Omnium," I can imagine setting the words to music, and subsuming time, then, not only in its relation to life and death but also in its relation to space and matter (inasmuch as time in music is measured). Stravinsky does this in his *Symphony of Psalms*, using Psalms 38, 39, and 150, much as Augustine in his *Confessions* uses Psalms 4, 41, and 138.[63] What Psalms would I use, or what three Psalms would I use, I wonder, if I were trying to commune like this with God and with others? Augustine's Psalms speak of light, of thirsting, of God knowing; Stravinsky's of crying out, of being heard, of music.

"Our relation to our fellow human beings is that of prayer, our relation to ourselves that of striving," Kafka says, "from prayer we draw the strength for striving."[64] These Psalms are prayer and seem to touch just that point where striving goes over into prayer and our relation with ourselves goes over into our relation with others. The Psalms I choose must be the ones that express my striving and that carry me over into prayer and into relationship with God and with human beings in spiritual friendship.

When I am feeling the loss of human friendship, I find myself calling out to God in the words like those of the Psalms, for they seem to express very well the "four perturbations of the mind,"[65] as Saint Augustine calls them, desire and gladness, fear and sadness. I find myself clinging to God and wanting to feel safe in God's sheltering care. The words of Psalm 91 of Sunday Night Prayer are mine then, "Lord, my refuge," and God's answer "I am with you."[66] I know this is the very Psalm the devil quotes to Christ in the desert, but I feel I am in the desert and am being tempted, not so much to presume on God as to think God is not enough for me. That is wisdom, to know God is enough. In *Plotinus or the Simplicity of Vision* Pierre Hadot says "The Plotinian experience constantly expresses itself in terms of light, brightness, transparency, brilliance, and illumination" and "insofar as the night of the Christian mystics corresponds to the exercise of faith, even to the point of becoming one with the suffering and crucified Christ, abandoned by the Father, it is obvious that all this is absent from Plotinus."[67] What leaves one vulnerable to this experience of night, it seems, is the willingness to share one's deepest life with other persons.

For Plotinus, "one single Life, simple and luminous, flows through all things," Hadot goes on to say. "It is enough to set aside the Forms, which conceal it as they express it, in order for this Life to make us feel its presence." I feel a nostalgia for this "simplicity of vision" when I am going through the ins and outs of human friendship. To say "God is enough for me" is in one way to hark back to this simplicity and to the fulfillment of Eros in inner peace, but to say "God is enough for me" after becoming vulnerable to the loss of friendship is to await the dawn with hope while still living in the night. "God is enough for me" becomes an expression of faith. Then again, as I discovered, the loss is of "it," not of "thou," and the night is "the happy night" (*la noche dichosa*).[68] In fact, if I think simply of living in "I and thou" and letting go of "I and it," I find again "the simplicity of vision."

Living in "I and thou" is living in "the simplicity of vision" and is the essence of love as friendship. There is a cost, nevertheless, and that is "I and it"—I have to let go of "I and it." That is the cost, for instance, of Augustine's vision with Monica. He has to let go of "it," responding to the call "Take and read" in his moment of conversion. He has taken the words as addressed to him, "Not in riots and drunken parties, not in eroticism and indecencies, not in strife and rivalry, but put on the Lord Jesus Christ and make no provision for the flesh and its lusts."[69] I too have to let go of "it." Are there words I can read as if addressed to me, "Take and read"? There are Martin Buber's words *I and thou*, as if he were saying "Not in *I and it* . . . but put on *I and thou*. . . ." I can see what it means in my human relationships, not letting go of relationship itself but letting go of the will "to have and to hold." It means releasing and being released, forgiving and being forgiven. Forgiveness can be the ongoing "I and thou" of a lost friendship.

Releasing another person from the past and being released myself, I am living in the "I and thou" of simplicity rather than the "I and it" of bitterness, and I have a changed relation with time, living in the eternal presence. I am free of the past and open to the future in virtue of the presence and "the simplicity of vision." If I were to try and express this in the language of the Psalms, I would use the words of Psalm 131, especially the middle lines,

> But I have calmed and quieted my soul,
> like a child at its mother's breast;
> like a child that is quieted is my soul.[70]

These are the words of a Gradual Psalm, a Song of Ascents. There is an ascent here to "the simplicity of vision" like that of Plotinus, although there is also a sense of passing through the dark night of loss to the simple light, of passing through complexity to simplicity, through blindness to vision. "I have calmed and quieted my soul." Still, the calm and the quiet come of returning to a center of stillness that was there all along. It is a matter of "believing in simplicity,"[71] as Goethe says, of believing in the simple vision that always brings me back into my center, for me the vision of a journey with God in time. That is my way of seeing time as "a changing image of eternity." For Plotinus himself the vision is one of repose in God, "alone with the Alone." For me the repose in God comes of seeing myself on a journey with God, even being carried by God.

"To believe in simplicity," I gather, is to live in the "I and thou" of the journey with God in time, holding myself open to "the mystery of encounter" while releasing others from the past and being released from it myself. Holding on to the past, as I am tempted to do, makes for complexity, pulls a long train behind me into the present. Letting it go leaves me free to be attentive to what is happening, to the signs pointing, to my own heart speaking, to the road opening in front of me, and being attentive is prayer, is enacting the "I and thou" with God. It leaves me open also to the very persons of my past as my relation with them becomes one of prayer, as Kafka says, rather than one of striving. I have to differentiate myself from them in going from striving to prayer, giving them over to God, but I gain in simplicity, I am more myself, they are more themselves.

Going from striving to prayer is like and unlike "having one's own death," as Heidegger says, and thereby having one's own life, a life "running ahead to its past, to an extreme possibility of itself that stands before it in certainty and utter indeterminacy."[72] When life opens up ahead of me all the way to death, he is saying, then I have a new past, the past of my life as a whole. I run ahead to the point where my whole life is past, even though that point, certain as it is, remains utterly hidden from me, and so I am able to relate to my life in a new way, to relate to my life as a whole. For me, however, the Archimedean point is not death so much as eternity, and so I want to go not from striving to striving but from striving to prayer. And I come not to be utterly alone in the face of death but to "I in them, and thou in me,"[73] as Christ says in the Gospel of John, to relate to the persons of my life through prayer and presence, "I in them" by way of "thou in me," I am in them by way of God in me.

"Presence to the self can thus be identical with presence to others," Hadot says, "on the condition that one has reached a degree of inwardness sufficient for discovering that the self, the true self, is not situated in corporeal individuality but in the spiritual world, where all beings are within each other, where each is the whole and yet remains himself."[74] My understanding of this situating of self in the spiritual world is that selfhood is in relationship, basically in "I and thou" with God and thence in "I and thou" with other persons. To say it "is not situated in corporeal individuality" is to say it is not situated in "I and it." So I come to something like Hillel's saying, "If I am here, everyone is here; if I am not here, who is here?"[75] If I am here, all who belong to my life are here, those "whom thou hast given me," as Christ says in the Gospel of John. "I desire that they also, whom thou hast given me, may be with me where I am."[76]

"God, then, is total presence," Hadot says, "the presence just as much of our self to itself as of individual beings to one another."[77] By standing in "I and thou" with God, I stand in "I and thou" with each and every person who belongs to my life, and vice-versa, by standing in "I and thou" with each of them I stand in "I and thou" with God. Here again, "attention is the natural prayer of the soul" and "our relation to our fellow human beings is that of prayer." The ascent of the soul to God is through "a conversion of attention."[78] For me it is like keeping your eyes on the road when you are driving an automobile, paying attention to the journey with

God in time and to the human encounters that occur on the journey. Every real presence is "a melody that sings itself,"[79] has its own inscape, its own inner landscape. But there is a unifying sense of presence, the pervading presence of God, and that is the sense that situates me on the mystic road of love. It is said that "mysticism is the recognition of the pure fact," because "the pure fact is mystery."[80]

Promise and forgiveness, the twofold relation to time in the Bible, commitment to the future and release from the past, as Hannah Arendt interprets them,[81] seem to arise out of the sense of eternal presence, out of recognition of "the mystical." I can see the meaning of marriage vows "forsaking all others"[82] (It is hard to be one of those forsaken others!) and yet I can see the hope in something like Tolkien's song "The Road Goes Ever On"—that is my road!—and I follow "until it joins some larger way where many paths and errands meet."[83] There is my commitment to the future and my release from the past, my willingness to let go of others and not hold them to the past, and yet my hope of meeting them again on "some larger way."

If I were trying to express this hope in the language of the Psalms, I would use the words

And now, Lord, what is there to wait for?
In you rests all my hope.[84]

It is the Psalm that ends with the words Stravinsky started with about crying out to God. Actually he composed his *Symphony of Psalms* from the end, starting with the last movement about music, then going on to the middle movement about being heard, and finally ending with the first movement about crying out.[85] My own sequence, starting with taking refuge in the Lord, then calming and quieting my soul, and finally waiting on God with hope comes and goes with a willingness to walk alone. This is the connecting insight, this attitude of willingness, not a will to walk alone that would exclude human company but a willingness to walk alone that welcomes companionship. If and only if I am willing to walk alone, I can see, then and only then am I capable of love as friendship. If and only if God is enough for me, then and only then am I capable of love.

It is something I have learned from Tolkien, this willingness to walk alone, seeing how his main character, Frodo, has at each turning point to be willing to walk alone, but as soon as he achieves this willingness he always finds human companionship. This last element, the finding that comes after letting go, is the hope that goes with the willingness. I am willing to walk alone with God, and yet I hope to find human companionship. I let go of a friend I have lost and yet I hold on to the friendship. I let go of the "I and it," let go of the human intercourse with the friend, and hold on to the "I and thou," hold on to the relationship with the friend. The letting go is the willingness; the holding on is the hope. May I hope then to find the friend again, to come again into touch?

That is certainly what Tolkien's story seems to imply. There is a coming into touch, nevertheless, in prayer, "our relation to our fellow human beings is that of prayer," and that goes back into the thought that God is enough for me. I could conclude, then, with being capable of love and friendship rather than with the meeting of friends. But let me be hopeful instead and conclude with the reunion of friends. "I in them, and thou in me" is a reunion in the spirit, but I may hope for reunion in the flesh. "And we shall meet again as friend and friend, and heart shall speak peace unto heart."[86]

Losing the "it" of a friendship, the intercourse of friend and friend, is like losing the journal where you have been writing your inmost thoughts. Your find your thoughts are scattered, and when you begin a new journal you cannot seem to regain the continuity you had before. You have bad dreams, like Frodo's "dark and despairing dreams that visited him in March and October during his last three years."[87] What if the silence continues? you ask yourself. You become fascinated with thoughts that seem to replace your former thoughts but seem less grounded in your life. Your dreams start to reflect the obsession and compulsion of these new thoughts. All the same, you find unhoped-for encounters, other friends who reappear in your life after a long absence, and that rekindles the excitement of the journey in time and seems to bring a new sense of continuity between past and future, despite all your letting go of the past.

It is possible to end up as Plotinus did in his last days, truly "alone with the Alone," according to "the terrible *pensée* of Pascal," as Hadot calls it, where Pascal says, "It is certainly very pleasant to relax in the company of our fellows! But they are as miserable and impotent as we are; they won't help us. We shall die alone. Therefore, we must act as if we were alone."[88] I want to think, though, as "our relation with our fellow human beings is that of prayer" that they are with us even when we are alone with God, and we can hope for an ending like Frodo's, not being all alone, as in his bad dreams, but being with our friends, as we sail into the West. I can count on the spiritual reunion, "I in them, and thou in me," but I may hope for a reunion where "I in them, and thou in me" becomes flesh.

I may hope, I say. I am answering Kant's question "What may I hope?" And the answer to that one depends, I can see, on the answer I give to his other two questions "What can I know?" and "What should I do?"[89] As I meditate on those questions and on the saying of Heraclitus, "Unless you hope, you will not find the unhoped-for,"[90] it occurs to me that I may be so set on hoping for reunion with a particular friend that I am not open to "the unhoped-for," another friend who makes an appearance in my life just at this time of loss. To receive what is given to me, as in that phrase "those whom thou hast given me," that is what I may hope! I have to pass from *espoir* to *esperance*, as Jean Giono says,[91] from hope to hopefulness, from a hope where I have set my heart upon a particular friend's love to a hopefulness open to the mystery of God's love.

Agape: Love as of God

"While I was so happy, a grey-bearded, ragged man, with a hewn face of great power and weariness, came slowly along the path till opposite the spring; and then he let himself down with a sigh upon my clothes spread out over a rock beside the path, for the sun-heat to chase out their thronging vermin. He heard me and leaned forward, peering with rheumy eyes at this white thing splashing in the hollow beyond the veil of sun-mist. After a long stare he seemed content, and closed his eyes, groaning, *The love is from God, and of God, and towards God.*"[92]

I've been meditating on these words from *Seven Pillars of Wisdom* by T. E. Lawrence for twenty years now, and I find ever more and more meaning in them. They do seem indeed the words of Holy Wisdom, my Ayasofya, of whom it is said in the Book of Proverbs, "Wisdom has built her house, she has set up her seven pillars."[93] Taking them as her words, I repeat them to myself, "The love is from God, and of God, and towards God," and I seem to come to an insight into love. I see the connection with Dante's ending in love in his *Paradiso*. I want to be able to say as he does at the end, I feel myself moved by "the love that moves the sun and the other stars."[94] Am I already moved by that love? Yes, I believe so—we love with a love we do not know, I have come to believe, we experience a deep loneliness that is not taken away in human intimacy, and there is a longing in that loneliness, a longing that becomes love, is love as longing, and is shared in love as friendship. And when an old friend comes back into my life, as just happened for me, and we share with each other the deep longing of our hearts, then we come to a vision, like Monica and

Augustine at Ostia, and we feel moved by a love that comes from God and goes to God.

But is all love encompassed in the love that is of God? It is, I want to say, on *the path taken by the soul of the dancer.*[95] Those words are from Kleist's essay "On the Marionette Theatre." As I read that amazing essay, I think of King David, "And David danced before the Lord with all his might."[96] As Kleist envisions marionettes, they have only one string attached, and it is attached to their center of gravity. So when they are drawn along a straight path their limbs describe circles. They move with a grace that is unconscious. To move like that we have to be in our own center of gravity.

Our center of gravity, however, corresponds to the fact that "We all have within us a center of stillness surrounded by silence." Our physical center corresponds to our spiritual center. Thus our soul should be in our center of gravity, according to Kleist, and then we would move with grace, but often it is not there and we are awkward. Ever since we became conscious of ourselves, self-conscious with "the knowledge of good and evil," we have been in exile from the garden of paradise. Grace goes with being unself-conscious or else at the other extreme with infinite consciousness, and "This is the point," Kleist says, "where the two ends of the circular world meet."[97] When he speaks of the circular world and its two ends meeting, I think again of the words, "The love is from God, and of God, and towards God." As I see it, we do have the possibility of living in our center, "a center of stillness surrounded by silence," and that center corresponds to "the still point of the turning world"[98] and to "the point where the two ends of the circular world meet."

There is a correspondence of center to center, of center of gravity to center of stillness, of center of stillness to the still point of the turning world. Is this metaphor or more than metaphor? For myself I can see the practice of the love of God means the practice of the presence of God, living in my center of stillness surrounded by silence. What, though, of the surrounding noise? Am I to live in my center of gravity and dance before the Lord with all my might? Am I to live at the still point of the turning world and be caught up in the love that moves sun and stars? Are all of these one and the same?

Let us begin with the surrounding noise. Using the old French word *noise*, the information theorist Michel Serres talks about background noise, the opposite of information, as the origin of all in his *Genesis*. He begins with "A Short Tall Tale,"[99] as he calls it, about being on the Sargasso Sea, ready to founder, and finding a noisy gathering of floating bottles, each with a message inside, and making himself a raft of them on which he makes his way back to Bordeaux. We survive by information, he seems to be saying, on a sea of noise. Certainly all the terms of information theory are here in his story, both information in the form of messages in the bottles and background noise in the form of the sea of bottles bumping together. It is far from "a center of stillness surrounded by silence," far and yet near. "We listen to our inmost selves," Martin Buber says, "and we do not know which sea we hear murmuring."[100]

Which sea do we hear murmuring? The sea of background noise, Serres says, and he illustrates, passing from auditory to visual images, with a story from Balzac about a painting by a mad painter, a chaotic painting called *La belle noiseuse*.[101] Here again we have that word *noise* with its meaning of "noise, noisy strife, quarrel" and its root in the Latin word *nausea*, "seasickness." There is in our times a fascination with chaos—witness the scientific studies of chaos such as Edward Lorenz's now famous little essay on "The Butterfly Effect" ("Does the Flap of a Butterfly's Wings in Brazil Set off a Tornado in Texas?").[102] The chaos is noise, strife, "hate," Serres says, and out of it comes music, harmony, love. *La belle noiseuse*, almost impossible to translate, is *noiseuse*, chaotic, and yet *belle*, beautiful.

When I am actually standing on the seashore and seeing waves breaking and hearing their thunder, I am not really thinking of chaos or even of background noise, for here the background becomes the foreground and blots out all else. It is a surrounding noise that is like a surrounding silence. "Background noise may well be the ground of our being," Serres says as he is talking about "Sea Noise." "It may be that our being is not at rest, it may be that it is not in motion, it may be that our being is disturbed."[103] Here he is like and unlike Saint Augustine saying "our heart is restless until it rests in you." I feel the restless movement of the heart in the restless movement of the sea. Is there rest in this restlessness? Just listening to the sea is restful. Is the divine presence in the surrounding noise as in the surrounding silence? I think of Elijah, and how "the Lord passed by . . . but the Lord was not in the wind . . . not in the earthquake . . . not in the fire." Then "after the fire" there was "a still small voice."[104] Is there "a still small voice" in or after the surrounding noise?

There is a peacefulness, just as there is in the surrounding silence when you are in your center of stillness. It is as if there were "a still small voice" in the noise as in the silence. "Wherever we are, what we hear is mostly noise," the composer John Cage says. "When we ignore it, it disturbs us. When we listen to it, we find it fascinating."[105] He says this, significantly, in a book called *Silence*. To encompass all my longings in the love of God I have to listen to the noise of my life. Cage is right. When I ignore it, it disturbs me. When I listen to it, I find it fascinating. The noise of my life, I begin to see, can become music, and the music of my life can become love.

What is the noise of my life? It is all the byways of my life, calling to me like Sirens. They unite into something like *La Belle Noiseuse*, the chaotic painting in Balzac's story. The mad old artist sees the figure he is painting as the passion of his life, and at first he will not show it to others. "Ah, love is a mystery," he says, "it lives only in the depths of the heart, and all is lost when a man says, even to his best friend: that is the woman I love."[106] I am that old man, that mad painter, and the image I am creating of the passion of my life is a beautiful figure to me, but to another, as to the young painter in the story, it may be "nothing but confused masses of colors."[107] Who is right? In the end the old man shows his masterpiece to others and they convince him there is nothing there. "Nothing! nothing!" he cries. "The work of ten years! What a crazy old fool I am!"[108] He is like Don Quixote on his deathbed, and he does die during the night, having burned his paintings. But is there really nothing? Do the byways of life simply diverge or do they converge onto the main road?

What then is the music of my life? It is words and music, like *musica* or *musike* in the ancient sense, words and music expressing my heart's desire, bringing unity out of multiplicity, out of the chaos of my life, information out of the background noise, as Serres says in his *Genesis*, information in the form of messages, "insight," the term I learned from my old teacher Bernard Lonergan, and "reasons of the heart," the term I learned from Pascal. Insight occurs when reasons of the heart become known to the mind. I see my life as one of gaining and sharing insight, expressing insight in words, expressing reasons of the heart in music. The link between words and music is the link between insight and reasons of the heart. *La Belle Noiseuse* becomes *La Belle Danseuse*.[109] Chaos becomes dance.

What then is the love of my life? Sometimes another person can answer that question for you better than you can answer it for yourself. I think again of my friend who wrote "I read in your eyes a sorrow too deep to express, a long lonely road that flickers through your being at the moment of our parting," and "Sometimes I think that you aren't really even seeing me at that moment, but that you are communing for a second with someone else." And I think again of the young Turkish woman who said, seeing my enthusiasm, "You are in love with Ayasofya." When the chaotic figure of *La Belle Noiseuse* comes into focus for me, I do believe, she will be Ayasofya, the figure of Holy Wisdom. There is something collective about the chaotic figure. It is "collective furor,"[110] Serres says. To bring it into focus, however, is individual. I emerge as an individual as my love finds its focus in the figure of Holy Wisdom. "There is a woman underneath,"[111] one onlooker says to another, looking at the beautiful foot emerging from the chaos of colors in the *La Belle Noiseuse*. The figure of the beautiful woman in Balzac's story is what is called "a strange attractor" in present-day studies of chaos. "A strange attractor, when it exists, is truly the heart of a chaotic system," Edward Lorenz says in *The Essence of Chaos*. "For one special complicated chaotic system—the global weather—the attractor is simply the climate, that is, the set of weather patterns that have at least some chance of occasionally occuring."[112] For me, in the chaos of my life, the strange attractor, I believe, is the figure of Ayasofya, and as I come to perceive her, to discern and follow her leading, I find myself emerging from chaos.

Time comes to birth out of background noise, according to Serres,[113] the word *temps* in French meaning both time and the weather. But eternity shows itself in time, I want to say, the mystery that "shows itself and at the same time withdraws," and that is how Ayasofya emerges, she shows herself and at the same time withdraws, leading me on. She shows herself as light, but why does she withdraw? I've written lyrics of a song, asking her

> Why is it dark at night?
> —a thousand stars
> are like a thousand suns!
> Why is it dark before me,
> if your light
> shines on my path?

I can know more
than I can tell
of light and darkness,
for if your eyes open,
there is light,
if your eyes close,
then there is dark,
but light inside my heart.

There are many echoes in those words: Olbers' paradox, a shining path, a tacit knowing, Ra's eye opening and closing, an inner light. What if I set the words to music?

I find, as I set it to music, that I have to name my poem, even if only by its opening words, "Why is it dark at night?" But I will give it a name, "Dark Light," with hints of infrared and ultraviolet and dark stars and the mystic "ray of darkness." I find a melody too, a simple pentatonic melody that leads back into itself with a rhythm that matches the rhythm of the words. And then I find a piano accompaniment, just a downbeat and an upbeat, the upbeat coming on the accent of the words rather than the downbeat, to create a sense of free rhythm. But I find two harmonies, one in broken sevenths, and another in broken tritones, the one in sevenths sounding romantic, the one in tritones strange, but as I play them over and over I am more at home with the sevenths and their feeling of confident hope .

There is an idea here of *the music of words*, that words call for music and music calls for words. This idea of the music of words, I think, belongs to poetics rather than linguistics, though there is a linguistic issue, Can music be mapped on language and language on music? I want to say Yes, so there is an ultimate unity of words and music, behind us in the far past and ahead of us in the far future. Anyway, here is the musical setting of these words:

Dark Light

Adagio

John S. Dunne (1996)

Why is it dark at night? a thou - sand stars are like a thou - sand suns!

Why is it dark be - fore me, if your light shines on my path? I can

know more than I can tell of light and dark - ness, for if your eyes o -

pen, there is light, if your eyes close, then there is dark, but light in - side my heart.

"In the beginning is not the word," Serres writes at the end of his *Genesis*. "One writes initially through a wave of music, a groundswell that comes from the background noise. . . . In the beginning is the song."[114] For me the opening words of the Gospel of John, "In the beginning was the Word," speak to the heart. In composing music I begin with the words. It is true, though, the music itself is "a groundswell that comes from the background noise." It comes from there to meet the words. Serres names the last chapter of his *Genesis* simply "Dream." For me the guiding dream here is "the meeting in a dream,"[115] as Borges calls the re-union of Dante and Beatrice. I do dream of reunion, as if there really were a dream dreaming us, like Dante's dream. It could be simply an example of Freud's interpretation of dreams as wish-fulfillment. Or it could mean that and more, a meeting of person and person that is a meeting of words and music, my words meeting the music that emerges like a wave from the background noise of my life.

"This is the point where the two ends of the circular world meet," Kleist's words seem to come true here. It is a meeting that occurs ever and again on what he calls "the path taken by the soul of the dancer." I long to meet again lost human friends, but my hope leads me into the unhoped-for, a meeting with Ayasofya, the figure of Holy Wisdom, and in my meeting with her my words of longing and questioning become song and song becomes dance. I connect words with my right hand (I am right-handed) and music with my left hand, my shadow side, but the two come together here, the two ends of my circular world meet as I meet Ayasofya.

"Does this mean we must eat again of the tree of knowledge in order to return to the state of innocence?" Kleist asks, for reading Kant had led him to despair of the intellect ever coming to truth. "Of course," replies his friend the dancer, "but that's the final chapter in the history of the world."[116] The first time we ate of the tree of knowledge we came to consciousness, Kleist is thinking; the second time we eat of it we will come to wisdom. For me meeting the figure of Holy Wisdom is an anticipation of that final chapter in the life of an individual. I think again of Solovyov and his poem "Three Meetings" where he describes his three encounters with Holy Wisdom, though he does not name her. His is a threefold experience of vision. Dante's is "the meeting in a dream." Mine is dream too and a kindling of heart, an illumining of mind. But it is this last, the kindling and illumining, more than dream or vision, that is the essence for us all, I believe, the "Dark Light," as I call it, showing us the way.

There is a kindling and an illumining, I find, in the meeting of words and music. In his foreword to his composition *Pierrot Lunaire*, Arnold Schoenberg says, "The performer's task here is at no time to derive the mood and character of the individual pieces from the meaning of the words, but always solely from the music."[117] For me it is the other way around, the words are the key to the interpretation of the music. Still, it is true, the music comes to meet the words like a wave from the sea of background noise. It comes as an unhoped-for response to the hope expressed in the words. Ayasofya is a "strange attractor," an unexpected figure emerging from the chaos of my life, of my divided heart, of my wandering eye. My heart is kindled, my mind is illumined, when I realize she is the one I love.

"We have to go on and make the journey round the world," Kleist says of paradise, "to see if it is perhaps open somewhere at the back."[118] Dante's "meeting in a dream" takes place in the earthly paradise and then Beatrice leads him on into the heavenly paradise. My own dream of reunion would be a kind of earthly paradise for me, but my meeting with Ayasofya, the kindling of my heart, the illumining of my mind, can lead me now on my own journey beyond the event horizon. It is as if I were "to go on and make the journey round the world to see if it is perhaps open somewhere at the back." But I may hope my journey will end like Dante's in being caught up in the love that pervades the whole universe, as I follow her gaze who sees "the whence of every where and when." Connecting my center of stillness with my center of gravity, like Kleist, and with the still point of the turning world, like Dante, I can make the two ends of my circular world meet. Living in my own center, I find myself living in the center that is everywhere in the hypersphere of the universe. It is Ayasofya for me ("You are in love with Ayasofya"), like Beatrice for Dante, who says,

I've seen the whence of every where and when.

But looking into her eyes, looking into human eyes that read in my eyes "a long lonely road that flickers through your being at the moment of our parting," looking into human eyes that see my eyes "communing for a second with someone else," I feel myself caught up in a longing, a loneliness, a love that moves us all, dancing and turning on our still point "like a balance wheel,"

The love that moves the sun and all the stars.[119]

I feel again the simple wonder of existence I used to feel as a child, lying on my back on a summer night, looking up at all the stars I could see. I wasn't asking the question then "Why is it dark at night?" but just feeling the wonder and wondering if there were many other worlds up there like our own. Now that I do ask "Why is it dark at night?" looking into the past and "Why is it dark before me?" looking into the future, the wonder of existence seems to be an answer. The longing, the loneliness, the love seem to climax in the joy of being on a journey with God in time.

The Mystic Road of Love

"On the road,"[1] Jack Kerouac's phrase for being on a journey, can describe also being on a journey in time and on a mystic road of love, an adventure that can be happy and sad, "beat" as in "beatific vision." I find it is not just a matter of letting go of "false hopes" or of "vain hopes and groundless fears," but instead of the hoped-for I have come upon the unhoped-for. Out of the chaos of life there has emerged "a strange attractor," the figure of Ayasofya.

There is a fairy tale by Goethe, "The Green Snake and the Beautiful Lily,"[2] that seems to cast light on this emergence. The Green Snake in the story is able to shape itself as a bridge over which others may cross the river and also to shape itself as a ring around others that turns into a ring of precious stones. The Beautiful Lily, on the other hand, turns the living into the dead and the dead into the living, doing this also to the Prince who loves her. It is a rather complex tale, but it comes to a happy ending in the resurrection of the Prince and his reunion with the Beautiful Lily. The role of sacrifice in the story goes not to the Prince but to the Green Snake who forms a ring around the dead Prince that allows him to come to life when it turns into a ring of precious stones. The Beautiful Lily then passes from her death-dealing role to her life-giving role and brings the Prince to life. Does the Green Snake correspond to the chaos of life, I wonder, and does the Beautiful Lily correspond to Ayasofya?

On the cover of the fairy tale, in the edition I am using, there is a painting by William Blake.[3] It is of a beautiful Eve, standing forth in the coil of the serpent, and it is clear from her look, one arm raised and the other stretched behind her, she has just awakened to the knowledge of good and evil while Adam is still unconscious, lying on the ground nearby. There is a wisdom that is death-dealing, the knowledge of good and evil, and there is a wisdom that is life-giving. The knowledge of good and evil I take to be the consciousness we have come to in the emergence and separation of the human race and of the individual. The death-dealing aspect is in the separation of the human race from other living beings and in the lonely separation of the individual from the rest of humanity. The life-giving wisdom is in the consciousness that comes with reunion.

If I connect the Green Snake in Goethe's fairy tale with the chaos of life and the Beautiful Lily with the figure of Ayasofya, then I am connecting the chaos of life with wholeness, the snake swallowing its tail, and the pattern emerging out of chaos with wisdom, a wisdom that encompasses death as well as life, the consciousness that goes with separation as well as with reunion. "Whether I can help I do not know," the Sage says in Goethe's story, "a single person cannot help, only one who joins with others at the right time."[4]

What is the chaos of life, and how does it relate to "the right time"? "Maybe these yellow arrows slanting in through the window were conscious, hoped for something better—and realized that their hopes were groundless, giving them all the necessary ingredients for suffering,"[5] Andrei reflects, gazing at the yellow sunrays, in Victor Pelevin's story The Yellow Arrow. Then he goes on to realize or remember he is on a train called the Yellow Arrow, speeding toward a wrecked bridge. It is a train that has no beginning, no end, and makes no stops. Here is the chaos of life. What then is the pattern emerging from the chaos, the "strange attractor"? Is it "the unhoped-for" as in that saying of Heraclitus I've been quoting, "Unless you hope you will not find the unhoped-for?" There is beauty in "these yellow arrows slanting in through the windows" even if there is no beauty in the dismal scene they arrive at. Have they come all the way from the sun to the earth for this?

At the end of the story Andrei does come upon "the unhoped-for." The train has unaccountably stopped, time itself has stopped, and he is able to get off and walk away, "and soon he could hear quite clearly sounds he'd never heard before—a dry chirping in the grass, the sighing of the wind and his own quiet steps."[6] I take it the Yellow Arrow is time, having no beginning or ending or stopping unless you make contact somehow with the eternal in life that can bring time to a stop. Wisdom is a consciousness of the eternal in time. It is at first death-dealing when it is only a consciousness of time, of being on the Yellow Arrow, but it becomes life-giving when it becomes awareness of the eternal in life that brings time to a stop. The knowledge of good and evil is a consciousness in which "time," as Heidegger says in *Being and Time*, is "the possible horizon for any understanding whatsoever of Being."[7] It changes to life-giving wisdom when we realize time is "a changing image of eternity."

What then is "the right time"? It is the point, I believe, where time intersects with eternity, where we touch upon the eternal in us and the way opens up before us. Three times in Goethe's story the Beautiful Lily hears it said, "The time is at hand,"[8] and though the Green Snake says it only once, the words seem to come ultimately from the Snake, as if they were coming out of the chaos of life into the light of wisdom. Something like that happens also in Pelevin's story when Andrei reads a friend's letter about time and the Yellow Arrow stops and time seems to stand still. I see my own "Setting Out" as coming at just such a moment, "Once upon a time of loss I set out on a mystic road of love." It is the eternal in us that lights up the road that goes ever on and on instead of dead-ending in a wrecked bridge, instead of ending, that is, simply in death. A time of loss can be the right time, for it is the time when I become aware of the transcendence of longing, how my heart is never satisfied with "I and it" and how loss is always of "I and it" rather than of "I and thou."

All the same, I want it, I fear its loss, I enjoy it, and I am sad to lose it. "I and it" belong to the wholeness of life, the snake swallowing its tail, as well as "I and thou." That is why there is "The Way Below," the low road of "I and it," as well as "The Way Above," the high road of "I and thou." Still, it is largely a matter of sacrifice. "What have you decided?" the snake is asked in Goethe's story. "To sacrifice myself before I am sacrificed,"[9] the snake replies. That is the way with "I and it," I can see, I have to sacrifice it. "We believe that we may meet again in a time to come," as Tolkien says, ". . . that will only be when we have both lost all we now have."[10]

Why? "To sacrifice myself before I am sacrificed," the snake's words, say to me to let go before it is taken away. I am led toward Meister Eckhart and his *Gelassenheit*, his "letting be." Letting it be is wisdom. There is a kind of pervasive joy in his writing, even though he is not always talking about joy, and it does seem to come from the wisdom that is able to let be. If letting be is the essence of being, as Reiner Schurmann suggests,[11] comparing Meister Eckhart and Martin Heidegger on *Gelassenheit*, then the "Why" here is clear, for we are down to bedrock, the essence of being. It is the essence of being and the essence of thinking. To let be is to be like God in the beginning saying "Let there be light." In fact, that has to be the fundamental letting be, letting there be light, from creating the world to kindling the heart and illumining the mind.

Letting light shine in the darkness is what I am doing on "The Way Below," letting light shine in the darkness of a human heart, coping with lack and loss and letting go. Following Broch's Virgil here, I seem to be working my way back through the Prologue of John's Gospel, starting with the line, "The light shines in the darkness, and the darkness has not overcome it," and working back to the opening line, "In the beginning was the Word."[12] "Let there be light!" I say in the darkness of my lack and loss, and the light does shine, letting go does seem to answer lack and loss as I go from unwillingness to willingness to walk alone. The light is in the letting be. At the same time it is also true to say, "and the darkness comprehended it not," my feelings of lack and loss do not understand letting be, for they are feelings of not having and they look to having, not to letting be. Having is the hoped-for; letting be is the unhoped-for.

"He was already willing, we may note, to go alone, would ask no one else to share the danger," Helen Luke comments on Frodo in Tolkien's story. "In this perhaps is a clue to the fate which had chosen him. He was that rare thing, a man willing to walk alone."[13] Lack and loss in a life may have a link with letting go, "a clue to the fate which had chosen him," as if my letting be, my willingness to walk alone, were the reason for my lack and my loss. My willingness is my Yes to the journey with God in time. So it is not just an acceptance of lack and loss but a consent to an all-consuming adventure with God, all-consuming because it encompasses my whole life, because it is with God, because "God requires the heart." My lack of human companionship, such as it is, my loss of contact with friends, may belong to "the fate which has chosen me," but it pales beside the excitement of the adventure with God.

You don't just choose a path in life, it seems, you discover it. Still, you do choose it, or you are called upon to choose it, and you can go through stages of choice, as Helen Luke describes them: first being chosen by a fate, then falling at times into the unconscious, being wounded by loss and pierced by dark knowledge, and finally coming to "the implacable day" when you have to choose for yourself to say Yes or No to the path that has opened before you. This is what is happening for me, I can see now, on "The Way Below," coming through lack and loss and letting go, to a clarity and a willingness to walk with God on a journey in time, an adventure that requires the heart just because it is a journey with God.

Being chosen by a fate, that is the mixed feeling of being chosen and of having a fate, the feeling that surrounds the element of necessity in a life, what you discover rather than simply choose about your life, but it becomes a matter of choice, of Yes or No, once you discover it. When I choose it, say Yes, really to God, then I change necessity into freedom, I become heart-free and heart-whole. I've been thinking of this and talking of this for years, usually quoting Dag Hammarskjold and his moment when he says "For all that has been — Thanks! To all that shall be — Yes!"[14] But now I see how my "Thanks!" and "Yes!" is an "I and thou" with God. If God were dead for me, as for Nietzsche, it would be an "I and it" with life, something much more lonely. As it is, in my willingness to walk alone I find myself unalone, in an "I and thou" which opens upon every "I and thou." I imagine myself walking alone or walking alone with God, but I find God always providing human presences in my life.

Falling into the unconscious, as Helen Luke calls it, using Jungian language, is a danger when I turn to these human presences to take away my loneliness. I can fall into an unconsciousness of being alone and of being alone with the Alone. What happens to me is a fall into what spiritual masters call an "attachment." I think of Saint John of the Cross and his image of a bird held by a thread. I echo his words in a song called "Letting Go":

> My soul held
> by just a thread
> cannot fly
> till the thread is broken:

Yes, it has been broken for me,
No, I am still held
by holding on
until I fly
by letting go,
and I am able to let go
only by turning
to the mystery of encounter,
for there is hope there
where soul meets soul.[15]

My "letting be" is a willingness to walk alone, but my "openness to the mystery" is a hope of human encounter.

Breaking the thread, nevertheless, can be an experience of being wounded by loss and pierced by dark knowledge. For me the thread is broken when I lose a friend to whom I am most attached, and I try to catch up with my loss by letting be and being open to the mystery that shows itself and withdraws. I am "pierced by knowledge of the dark,"[16] Helen Luke's phrase, insofar as "One always learns one's mystery at the price of one's innocence"[17] (Robertson Davies). I learn my mystery at the price of my innocence here, being pierced by the dark knowledge that is spoken of in the Gospel of John, "but Jesus did not trust himself to them, because he knew all men and needed no one to bear witness of man; for he himself knew what was in man."[18] My mystery is my journey with God in time, and I am learning here the loneliness of the journey, learning really how the mystery "shows itself and at the same time withdraws" in human relations, and yet learning nonetheless to be open and remain open to the mystery of encounter.

"After such a wounding the days of instinctive choosing are over," Helen Luke says. "For every choice after this we must bear conscious responsibility."[19] Still, when it actually comes to it, though I am conscious and responsible, it is as if I were chosen rather than choosing, as in the words of the Gospel of John, "You did not choose me, but I chose you."[20] When I say "Thanks!" and "Yes!" I am responding to "the word beyond speech" calling me to the journey with God in time. "At last with an effort he spoke, and wondered to hear his own words," Tolkien says of Frodo, "as if some other will was using his small voice." *I will take the Ring*, he said, *though I do not know the way.*[21] So it is for me, I will go with God on the journey in time, though I do not know the way.

It is because I do not know the way that I need a guide, someone to hold the light for me on the low road, like Dante's Virgil, and on the high road, like Dante's Beatrice. I have chosen Broch's Virgil as my guide on the low road of lack and loss and letting go and Ayasofya herself as my guide on the high road of learning to love. And now I turn to her as I enter upon the high road. Originally I had thought of a human friend as my Beatrice, but then I realized Beatrice could guide Dante only because she had become a wisdom figure after death. An earthly friend cannot be a Beatrice, though a spiritual friendship can be a sharing of the journey. Letting earthly friends be and be friends is essential for me, I can see now, and goes with letting Ayasofya be my guide, and letting there be light on my path.

Let there be light! But how am I to relate to Ayasofya? By prayer as invocation ("Wisdom of God, be with me, always at work in me"). By prayer as attention to the encounters of my life, to the signs, to my heart speaking, to the way opening before me. There is thus a to-and-fro with her, a give and take. The "to" or the "give" is in the invocation; the "fro" or the "take" is in the attention. *Let there be light!* It is the "inner light" that shines on my path, the inner light that gives enlightenment and guidance and assurance. I find myself reciting the words of Saint Teresa, "Nada te turbe, nada te espante . . ." as if they were the words of Ayasofya herself giving me that enlightenment and guidance and assurance in dark times when I need it the most. I relate to her as to the inner light. *Poetry in the Dark Ages*, the title of a lecture by Helen Waddell,[22] describes very well the work of Ayasofya in our own dark times, providing we take poetry seriously, "crediting poetry," as Seamus Heaney says, as "an order where we can at last grow up to that which we stored up as we grew."[23] Learning to love is just that, growing up at last to the love we stored up as we grew. The "Yes!" here, "an order where we can at last grow up," is inseparable from the "Thanks!" "to that which we stored up as we grew." Loving God, thinking of God with joy, I am as willing to be on a journey with God in the future as I am thankful for being on a journey with God in the past. Letting be, I am learning to be and let be, to let friends be and be a friend. "We are hindered by cleaving to time," Meister Eckhart says. "Whatever cleaves to time is mortal."[24] I am hindered by cleaving to my past with friends, wanting the future to be like the past. My "Thanks!" and my "Yes!" is a loving that is a letting be. I am learning to love by letting time past and future be.

As I meditate on those words of Meister Eckhart, "We are hindered by cleaving to time. Whatever cleaves to time is mortal," I begin to understand the cryptic words I found in *The Yellow Arrow*:

> He who has cast off the world has likened it to
> yellow dust. Your body is like unto a wound, and you
> are like unto a madman. This entire world is a yellow
> arrow which has pierced you through. The Yellow Arrow
> is the train on which you ride toward a ruined bridge.[25]

Those words describe how everything becomes mortal when you cleave to time. When I let go of time past and future, when I let time be, I come upon the eternal in us. *It is the wisdom of love that "I and it" is passing, and "I and thou" is lasting.* That is the insight I have come to. As I walk in the wisdom of love then, I feel at peace in spite of all lack and loss. I am like the man at the end of *The Yellow Arrow.* I have escaped the Yellow Arrow that cleaves to time and makes everything mortal, and I begin to "hear quite clearly sounds" I'd "never heard before—a dry chirping in the grass, the sighing of the wind and" my "own quiet steps" as I walk with God in time.

All the same, I have feelings about "I and it" that won't go away. "What shall I do," one of the Desert Fathers was asked, "for the passions of the soul have dominion over me?" And the answer came, "Verily, this is love's road."[26] Helen Waddell reports this story, and it reminds me of her translation of Alcuin, "No mountain and no forest, land or sea, shall block love's road, deny the way to thee. . . . Yet why must love that's sweet so bitter tears beget?"[27] If it is true, as I believe, we love with a love we do not know, then "the passions of the soul" and the "bitter tears" that love begets are indeed "love's road." The wisdom of the desert here is in the words of the old Bedouin, "The love is from God and of God and towards God," and so the passions of the soul and the bitter tears too are "from God and of God and towards God," the deep loneliness we feel too and the longing in that loneliness. "Love's road" is the road of coming to know the love we do not know. It is my mystic road of love.

But the bitter tears, the passions of the soul, the deep loneliness, the longing are like the roar of a lion, if we think of the heart as *coeur de lion*, "heart of a lion," or lionheart as in Richard the Lionhearted, Richard Coeur de Lion. "The lion roars at the enraging desert,"[28] Wallace Stevens writes. It is the roar of unfulfilled longing, the roar of frustrated love, the roar of loving with a love we do not know. The lion roars in "the still desert of the Godhead," as Meister Eckhart calls it, "where never was seen difference, neither Father, Son, nor Holy Spirit, where there is no one at home, yet where the spark of the soul is more at peace than in itself."[29] Our heart of a lion roars at this solitude and yet comes to be at peace there. My heart roars with unrequited longing but comes to peace in letting be.

The lion roars at the enraging desert,
Reddens the sand with his red-colored noise,
Defies red emptiness to evolve his match.[30]

These lines of Wallace Stevens are from his "Notes Toward a
Supreme Fiction." If we let go of all our notions of God, un-
knowing all we know, undoing all our fictions, we find ourselves
in "the still desert of the Godhead." It is lonely there but lonely
with love and longing. That is how it is for me, that is how I
redden the sand with my red-colored noise. But there is an oasis
there in that desert, the Well at the World's End, according to the
story by William Morris.[31] I roar at the enraging desert and defy its
red emptiness, but the answering silence challenges me, calling
me to the oasis,

There is a lion heart in us
that roars at the enraging
desert of our solitude,
the still surrounding desert
of the Godhead there
where never was seen difference
of you and I,
where no one is at home,
yet where our spark of soul
is more at peace than in our self,
for we find our oasis there,
love changing us
into the things we love,
returning all the things we lost.

Song and Dance Cycles

Years ago my friend Henri Nouwen introduced me to *The Green Child*, a novel by Herbert Read, and I have included here the lyrics I have written for a musical version while working on this book. It was performed on November 24 and 25, 1997, in the chapel of Lewis Hall at Notre Dame.

A man returns, according to the story, after a very full life, to the village where he grew up and there he meets a woman, the Green Child, a numinous figure who seems to belong to another world. They journey together up the village stream, mysteriously flowing back to its source, and find their way into the world of underground caverns from which she comes, thus passing from air through water into earth. The ending of the story is rather ominous, as a friend of mine, John Gerber, once said, the bodies of the man and the woman turning to crystal after their death like stalagmites and stalactites, and so I thought to transform the story here somewhat with a hint of resurrection and of eternal life.

Also some years ago I went with my friend Maryanne Wolf to a place called World's End at Hingham in Massachusetts, thinking of the novel by William Morris *The Well at the World's End*. I have included here also the lyrics for a musical version I wrote while working on this book. It was performed on April 9 and 10, 1997, in the chapel of Lewis Hall at Notre Dame.

At world's end there is a well, according to the story, that can heal you of sorrow and restore you to a happy life. So people who have gone through loss and sadness will say "I must drink of the Well at the World's End." But there are those who say the well is only a story or at best an image of what you must do to recover from sorrow and come to a happy life. All the same, according to the story, you must have courage to drink of the well. And that is just what the man and the woman have and do in this tale. In my musical version I end with them drinking of the well and starting for home. Having tasted the water of the well, they feel the joy of being heart-free, of letting themselves be and letting God be, and they begin now to live in wandering joy, heading for home but wondering if anything can ever be the same.

THE GREEN CHILD

Prelude (Chorus)
Once upon
a time of loss
I set out on a mystic
road of love.

and I am able to let go
only by turning
to the mystery of encounter,
for there is hope there
where soul meets soul.

Lost Horizon Found (Olivero)
My life is journey,
and the peace of presence
is my company,
but then I've yearned
for human presence,
and I've found
and lost the prospect
of a friendship of the soul,
or feared I lost it,
but still heart goes out to heart,
and I may find the way again,
Yes, in the presence
on my way, my journey,
is my lost horizon found.

Eternal Return (Olivero)
Where is the dancing?
Where is the way?
I come from distance
and I go to intimacy
to escape the sense of time
and live in the eternal
essence of all things
—that is my one desire,
but it is essence
that impels me to return
here now where my own
        sense
of I was liberated first
in singleness that has become
my lasting truth of life.

Letting Go (Siloen)
My soul held
by just a thread
cannot fly
till the thread is broken:
Yes, it has been broken for me,
No, I am still held
by holding on
until I fly
by letting go,

The Green Child (Siloen)
An unknown life
draws you to love another
as if other of another world,
a symbol unresolved
of earthly radiance
and yet unearthly,
mother and child,
wisdom's figure

but a woman to herself
that longing always goes
    beyond
—so when you leave,
you leave her;
when you come back,
you come back to her.

The Road I Know
    (Olivero & Siloen)
The road I know
goes ever on and on
still after loss
and can rejoin
the other roads of life
I had not taken
and not even hoped
to find and walk again,
life's main chance
—I believed the presence
was enough for me
which is enough for me
when I walk on
beyond the road I know.

Water Dance (Chorus)
We go down
into the mystery
of water flowing
to its source.

No Fear (Siloen)
No fear,
no false hope,
no untoward desire,

no sadness
settle in your heart
to take away your peace,
for all is passing,
only One unchanging,
—waiting
comes to all fulfillment,
—holding to the One
you will lack nothing,
One alone
enough for you.

Loss of Self
    (Olivero & Siloen)
Loss of self
I fear in all I fear,
but I believe I live
after the dreadful has occurred
—it will not darken your heart
but will teach you wisdom
by the guiding,
by the guarding,
by the inner light,
for love usurps fear
not so you feel unafraid
but you know something
    stronger,
love the pure direction,
from and of and toward.

The Cloud of Forgetting
    (Olivero)
There is a cloud that comes
between the soul and its desire,

unknowing all we know,
a cloud that comes also
between the soul and all
    besides,
forgetting and not just
    forgetting,
letting go of sadness rather,
like the people I saw on
    the Amazon
who cannot hold on to
    their sadness
—I can hold on too well
to my sadness when it is all
I have of memory,
but I know to unknow
and I remember to forget.

Homing Love (Siloen)
We all have in us
a center that is still
surrounded by a silence
that is presence,
for desire can go in circles
as it mimes desire,
or go as straight
as heart to heart,
or spiral as we come to
    know
of love unknown
and come to rest
in our unrest
with homing love
of One alone.

Dreaming Time
    (Olivero & Siloen)
This is a dreaming time
when I rush off,
hope in pursuit of hope,
abandon will
for simple willingness,
abandon hope
for simple hopefulness,
—I walk alone
and hope to meet
someone, something:
my willingness is to walk
    on alone,
my hope to walk in love.

Earth Dance (Chorus)
We go down
into the heart of earth
to learn to love
and be heart-free.

Love's Distance
    (Olivero & Siloen)
Must it be
—the distance
between you and me
of mind and mind?
It must be
—love is our
consent to distance,
willing and unwillingness
of heart and heart!

It must be
—love's road
is our hope
of intimacy if unbodily
of soul and soul!

Infinite Longing (Siloen)
Infinite longing
is my recourse now,
to open my will to infinity,
abandon myself to the love
that places me in life and time,
but faith my faith is there is
    hope
of being capable of loving,
friendly to myself
and gentle in my
    disappointment,
—here is willingness
and here is hope,
because heart speaks to heart
and one heart goes out to
    another
undeterred by all between.

Mortmain (Olivero)
You have set before me
life and letting go
and death and holding on,
mortmain,
therefore I choose life,
I choose wisdom
rather than despair of love,

resentment,
desperately seeking
to be first in someone's heart,
for wisdom seems indeed a
    choice,
a Yes to Something
or Someone who can always
be first in my own heart.

Letting Be I Pray (Siloen)
For all that has been
between us—Thanks!
And all that has been
will be once again
by letting be I pray
while letting be,
for prayer is waiting
on the showing
and withdrawing,
playing hide-and-seek
with mystery
of being other and the same.

Being Oned
    (Olivero & Siloen)
To all that shall be—Yes,
we meet again I hope
upon the road ahead,
for hopes and fears are met
there in uncertainty,
for being there
is being possible
—Do not seek love.

Love will find you.
Seek instead love's road
and death's fulfillment on
    the road
to being oned.

Soul Dance (Chorus)
I walk alone
and unalone
—You are walking
with me on the way.

Love's Direction (Olivero)
I am intact
after my sorrow
that could have destroyed me
—a way of love
I found I loved I lost
along my life's meridian:
to have and not to hold,
that is time's arrow,
but to be and to let be
is love's direction,
where we come from
and where I am going now.

Figure and Ground (Siloen)
The figure and the ground
can be reversed,
the lonely figure I am
and the ground the mystical,
not how things are
but that they all exist,

the wonder that I saw
as I lay gazing
at the summer stars,
for everything speaks
and speaks of existence
and existence is divine,
and so my lone existence
is of wonder and divine.

The Way Above (Olivero)
I lose myself
in this dark wood of loss,
and in the middle still
of time's adventure
I have met in twilight
figures of my nightmare
who forbid my passage
but who disappear in the light,
—so I have found my guide
who knows the way below,
and if this and the otherworld
are really only one world,
I may find also the One
who knows the way above.

Whole Love (Siloen)
Whole love is greater
than a sum of loves,
and presence greater
than a sum of wishes,
—wholeness is the holiness,
to love with all my heartache
and with all my soulsickness,

to dance with all my might
because I know love
greater than which none
   can be
conceived with all my mind,
I know love is requited
by love knowing love.

Crystal Dance (Chorus)
I dance alone
and unalone
—You are dancing
with me on the way.

THE WELL AT THE WORLD'S END

Prelude
If you have tasted
of sorrow, you must
drink of the well
at world's end.

The Captive Heart
I wonder what tale
we have fallen into loving
with a love we do not know
of gazing and of praying,
of attention of the soul
in this direction we are looking
to a happy ending of sad
   endings,
but unconscious of
   beginning
the path integral
of love's direction,
happy as reunion,
sad as separation —
No, the captive heart is sad,
the happy ending is heart-free.

Coeur de Lion
There is a lion heart in us
that roars at this enraging
desert of our solitude,
the still surrounding desert
of the Godhead there
where never was seen
   difference

of you and I,
where no one is at home,
yet where our spark of soul
is more at peace than in
   our self,
for we find our oasis there,
love changing us
into the things we love,
returning all the things we lost.

Heartbeat
Perpetual the motion
of love's blood
we know in its great circle
from God and to God,
by heartbeat to heartbeat,
and all we know of love
and blood is less
than all that is unknown,
a heart divided by a wall,
unloved, unloving and
   unlovely,
longing to be understood
   in full,
if there were someone,
we would have support from
   every side,
we would have God.

Heartsease
Our heart is restless
with the story of our soul,

of wandering away
and then in fear and sadness,
and desire and gladness,
finding our way home
again by turning
and again by telling,
we are having once again
the highlife of our time,
until our heart can rest
in You by listening to You
as You are telling us
our story in repose.

Heart's Desire

An earthly friend I know now
cannot be my Beatrice, my
    Laura,
only Ayasofya can,
for the balance is so delicate
that a butterfly can spread its
    wings
and set off a tornado far away
where there are the balances
    and the periods,
but Wisdom is a strange
    attractor
coming out of chaos where
    we are
and what we hear is mostly
    noise
and we ignore and it disturbs
but if we listen it is fascinating,
for we are in love with
    Ayasofya,

our changing image of
    eternity.

The Road to Love

I have lost and found
and lost again—
Shall I then find
the lost once more?

The Thinking Heart

"I know who I am,"
    as Don Quixote says,
"I've been enchanted,"
"I was mad, and now I'm
    sane"
and thinking with my heart
a new life has begun,
a renaissance of sense and
    spirit,
after going through a night
of dark undreaming,
I can see the way of
    possibility
where words and music
and all friendship lost and
    found,
the bite of fear and care
    renewed,
are integral path integral.

Single Life

The single life I know is
    prayer,
the to-and-fro with God,

or utter loneliness with
  Wisdom,
where to be alone
with the Alone
is to be unalone
though lonely
for a human presence—
It is Wisdom's mystery I
  know
to show herself in human
  form
and at the same time to
  withdraw,
and it is mine I see
to let be and be open to her
  mystery
and to let there be light.

Dollhouse

Our only string attached
is to the center of our gravity
where we are moveable by
  grace,
unconscious love is our
  direction,
and the mystical our path
is taken by the dancer's soul
where grace appears most
  purely
when it is at unawares
or when there is no
  unawareness left,
and so we taste again of
  knowing

and unknowing good and evil
to love and love in return
at this point where the two
  ends
of the circular world meet.

Soul House

A child destroys
the toys—
where is the soul?
We cannot sleep,
the soul is hiding,
not allowing us to dream,
or to know more
than we can tell
when we are trying to tell all;
we cannot see beyond
event horizons
where the world soul hides
—You are soul of my soul
and of the universe!

Divine Conceit

By relating to myself
and willing then to be myself
I am grounded transparently
in something greater than
  myself
or any supreme fiction I
  conceive
    that must be abstract,
    that must change,
    that must give pleasure,
No, I let go of abstract,

of change, of pleasure,
I unknow all I know
to love You unknown,
to know You in love,
thinking back to thanking
    that I am.

The Road to Utterbol
"Not first
in nobody's heart,"
You will always
be the first in my heart.

The Handless Maiden
Eternal the recurrence
of the same events in dream
that occupy my soul's
    attention,
for she raises her hands
without realizing she can
and then discovers them
as if by chance because
attention is the natural prayer
    of soul
and her attention to the other
in the mystery of encounter
leaves her own reach,
her own grasp at unawares
until she sees her hands
raised up in prayer.

The Fisher King
Time's arrow pierces
and your body is a wound

and you a madman
on your way toward death
unless time also heals,
the arrow can be drawn
and contemplated,
    calculated
like the little arrows,
waves and particles
of light and matter
in sum over histories—
What is the sum?
You are the One
in us and in the universe.

God of the Shining Sky
I love God of the shining sky
who leads into the desert
where heart speaks to heart
of universal reconciliation,
where bread nourishes
but does not satisfy desire,
where water from the well
takes sorrow and leaves joy
no one can take away,
but I remain heart-free,
letting myself be,
letting God be,
I can live in wandering
joy without a cause.

Urfaust
I am here now
therefore I think of time
and am caught up

in dreams of relativity,
exchanging poetry
for truth in lending
the time being
where now ever changes,
making soul
the gift, the theft,
and the exchange
always the womanly,
the singing timelessness
of heart's desire.

Listen Zarathustra
Inertia here
arises from mass there,
the boundary is
there is no boundary
but return to the beginning
where love is alive
and all alive to love,
for in the end
the human essence
in us individual,
in man and woman,
in the sum of our relations
must return
alone with love alone.

The Road to the Well
We find our way
to the world's end
where we know
all our loves are one love.

The Dry Tree
To be outside
the human circle,
looking in
from solitude,
is death until
death parts us,
love until
love joins us,
natural as prayer,
conscious as attention
in the one direction
we are never looking
—Oh but to be there
and let be there!

At the Well
(**Man at the Well**)
Do I stand by the well
and die of thirst? Yes,
a sage's life is simple,
insight and the message,
Yes, I see the way,
withdraw into the
    solitude
and then return
into the human circle,
but is this enough for me?
—if You are
and I am,
if You and I are one,
if your love and my love
are one love of the One.

(**Woman at the Well**)
Drink of me, it sings,
if only with your eyes,
and I will live in you,
if only in your heart
—my eyes are yearning
toward the smiling dark,
the bright unsmiling
one who shows
and then withdraws
—if You are
and I am,
if You and I are one,
if your love and my love
are one love of the One.

and found we could feel
     support,
and so we came to know
God sensible to heart,
but still we search
for bedrock of mind at
     wit's end,
and we walk together now
in the woods at world's
     end,
but all we see now
is the beauty and the golden
     light—
Is this wit's end?
Is this world's end?

World's End
We searched for God
and found only our
     searching,
but we leaned on God

The Road Home
We found our way
to the world's end
where we know
all our loves are one love.

A Note on the Dante-Riemann Universe

I

"At the still point of the turning world,"[1] that is how T. S. Eliot describes the inner center of Dante's world. It is a world that has an uncanny likeness to the world of modern physics as described in the theory of relativity, a hypersphere of Riemann's multidimensional geometry. There is the sphere of the visible universe, having the earth for us as its observational center, and there is the sphere invisible to us, having God at its center. These two spheres, like hemispheres, correspond to those of general relativity, the visible universe bounded by the event horizon, and the sphere beyond having an intense point of light at its origin that is the beginning of time. The *primum mobile* is the common boundary of the two spheres in the cosmology of *The Divine Comedy*, and "the event horizon" is their common boundary in the cosmology of general relativity.

There is a rival cosmology in modern physics and that is based on the quantum theory. It is the idea of "the wave function of the universe" and it goes with "the many worlds interpretation" of quantum mechanics. I say "rival" but the two have been welded together by Stephen Hawking and others.[2] Yet it may be possible, I think, to bring together quantum theory and relativity theory in *one world*. How? By taking matter as a dimension along with space and time.

Is matter a dimension? If time can be considered a dimension alongside the three dimensions of space, can matter also be considered a dimension? Length and time and mass all change in motion, according to relativity, length contracting, time dilating, mass increasing. I wonder then if all three are dimensions and constitute not just a space-time continuum but a manifold of space and time and matter. Some forty years ago I summoned up my courage and wrote to Erwin Schrödinger, asking if he thought the idea might be workable. I got a one sentence reply, "Matter is not a dimension," or it may have been "Mass is not a dimension." Anyway the reply was peremptory, and I laid the idea aside. Much has happened in the meantime, however, and I thought I might raise the question again.

When we say space and time are dimensions, we think of matter as what is *in* the dimensions, and the question is *where* it is and *when* it is, but if we say matter itself is a dimension along with space and time, then what is *in* the dimensions? *Events*, I suppose. What events? Light rays, I imagine, and particle trajectories, if we speak of time in relation to space and matter. Light rays lead to the idea of a spacetime continuum, and light rays and particle trajectories to that of a manifold of space and time and matter.

"Everything that exists is situated," Max Jacob says in his preface to *The Dice Cup*, his prose poems. "Everything that's above matter is situated; matter itself is situated."[3] Everything he means that exists in the physical world. He is speaking only of existence, not of transcendence, which cannot be situated. Everything that is above matter in the physical world—life and intelligence, I suppose— is situated in space and time. Matter itself is situated in space and time. *But does matter situate?* That is the question.

It does on the large level by warping or curving space, according to general relativity, and it does on the quantum level as well, as waves it situates and as particles it is situated. I think of Clifford's "Space-Theory of Matter," outlined already in the nineteenth century, using ideas of Riemann and saying space is curved and "this property of being curved or distorted is continually being passed on from one portion of space to another after the manner of a wave."[4] To say time is a dimension is essentially a space-theory of time, I think, and to say matter is a dimension is essentially a space-theory of matter.

II

Matter on the scale of waves and particles is usually described by a wave function ψ that is a function of space $\psi(x, y, z)$ or a function of space and time $\psi(x, y, z, t)$. What I have in mind is to take the wave function as a function of space and time and matter $\psi(x, y, z, t, m)$. The spacetime continuum comes from generalizing the equation for a light ray $r = ct$, and so I suppose the manifold of space and time and matter will come from generalizing the DeBroglie formula for the wavelength of matter waves $\lambda = h/mv$, where h is Planck's constant and mv is momentum. That is because each coordinate has to have the dimension of length in the formula for the line element ds. There is indeed a mass parameter in the wave equations of quantum theory, a fifth term in addition to the four of space and time, and it is related in each instance to the DeBroglie wave length.[5]

If I may be allowed one essential mathematical formula here, let me use the formula Riemann himself gives in his Inaugural Lecture for the line element of his universe,[6]

$$ds = \sqrt{\textstyle\sum dx^2} \,/(1 + \frac{\alpha}{4} \textstyle\sum x^2)$$

where the x are the coordinates of space, x and y and z, and α is the curvature of space. If $\alpha = 0$ this reduces back to ds in flat space. Although he supposes three dimensions here, Riemann remarks that the formula is valid for any number of dimensions, and we shall have to take advantage of that fact to interpret it in the light of relativity and quantum theory. From relativity we will have to take the x to include a fourth dimension, $x_4 = ict$, the dimension of time where t is time and c is the velocity of light and $i = \sqrt{-1}$, and from quantum theory we will have to take the x to include a fifth, $x_5 = \lambda = h/mv$, the DeBroglie formula for the wavelength of matter. There is a fifth dimension in the Kaluza-Klein unified field theory, although it is not interpreted as mass or matter. It is a fifth dimension in the curved space of gravitation, and there is this similarity, the fifth dimension according to Klein is on the quantum scale.[7]

If we say the curvature of space is due to large masses, such as that of earth and the moon and the sun, what is the relation of these masses to those of waves and particles? Large scale is related to small scale, according to this formula, as curvature α to fifth dimension x_5. It is possible, using x_5 then, to unite quantum theory and general relativity in a single metric ds of curved space in five dimensions. I use this formula for ds from Riemann's Inaugural Lecture because it is particularly simple and general, though we could use this same procedure with other known metrics of curved space.

We can see that Σx^2 represents a sphere, or really a hypersphere, in five dimensions. We can take it to be the hypersphere of the universe. Actually we can say with Einstein[8] that the universe is spherical if the curvature is positive ($\alpha > 0$), Euclidean if it is null ($\alpha = 0$), and pseudospherical if it is negative ($\alpha < 0$). Einstein's notation here is z instead of α for curvature, and he writes r^2 instead of Σx^2.

Summing up, we can say matter on the quantum scale is represented by the DeBroglie wave length λ, and this variable can serve as a coordinate. Matter on the large scale is represented by the curvature of space α. These two together, matter coordinate

λ and curvature α, define a metric, as above where we used Riemann's original formula from his Inaugural Lecture. A four-dimensional curved space can be embedded in a five-dimensional flat space. And thus the curvature α and the matter coordinate λ can be geometrically related. So we can say it is the matter coordinate and the curvature of space that together define matter as a dimension. What is more, if we can suppose a link between our matter coordinate and the curvature of space, we can expect a link also between matter waves and gravitational waves.[9]

Does this lead to one world rather than many worlds? I think it does.[10] There is an economy in the idea of a matter coordinate that seems to imply many frameworks rather than many worlds and thus to leave us with essentially *one world*.

Notes

Preface

1. Friedrich Nietzsche, *Thus Spake Zarathustra*, trans. with a preface by Walter Kaufmann (New York: Modern Library, 1995), p. xix.

2. William J. Broad, "Earth's Core Found to Be Spinning on Its Own" in *New York Times* for Thursday, July 18, 1996, pp. A 1 and A 9.

3. See p. oo.

4. The Buddhist-Christian dialogue was on monastic education in Buddhism and Christianity and was held at Kalamazoo from July 11 to 14, 1996. My talk was "Love's Mind: the Christian Monastic Education" and was on Saturday, July 13, 1996. Arthur Zajonc's book is *Catching the Light: The Entwined History of Light and the Mind* (New York, Oxford: Oxford University Press, 1993).

5. T. S. Eliot, *The Three Voices of Poetry* (Cambridge: Cambridge University Press, 1954). The first voice is the personal voice, the second is that of the poet addressing an audience, and the third is that of characters in a drama.

Setting Out

1. See below "Prelude" in lyrics for "The Green Child."

2. J. R. R. Tolkien, *The Adventures of Tom Bombadil* (Boston: Houghton Mifflin, 1963), pp. 57–60 (cf. p. 9).

3. Romans 14:7 (RSV).

4. Tolkien, *The Lord of the Rings* (London: George Allen & Unwin, 1969) (one volume edition), p. 1010.

5. Martin Heidegger, *Poetry, Language, Thought*, trans. Albert Hofstadter (New York: Harper & Row, 1971), p. 4.

6. Tolkien, *The Lord of the Rings*, p. 1011.

7. Ibid., p. 1067.

8. Ibid., p. 1069.

9. Deuteronomy 6:4 (RSV).

10. Heidegger, *The Concept of Time*, trans. William McNeill (Oxford U.K. & Cambridge U.S.A.: Blackwell, 1992), p. 11E. Jacques Derrida, *The Gift of Death*, trans. David Wills (Chicago & London: University of Chicago Press, 1995), p. 82.

11. Romans 14:7–9 (RSV).

12. Plato, *Timaeus* 37d (my translation).

13. Matthew 22:37; Mark 12:30; Luke 10:27 (RSV).

14. William Wordsworth, "Preface to Lyrical Ballads" in *William Wordsworth*, ed. Stephen Gill (Oxford & New York: Oxford University Press, 1990), p. 611.

15. Franz Kafka, *The Penal Colony*, trans. Willa & Edwin Muir (New York: Schocken, 1964), pp. 67–134. Apuleius, *Metamorphoses*, ed. & trans. J. Arthur Hanson (Cambridge, Mass.: Harvard University Press, 1969), vol. 2, pp. 299–305. See André-Jean Festugière, *Personal Religion among the Greeks* (Berkeley & Los Angeles: University of California Press, 1954), pp. 68–84.

16. Marija Gimbutas, *The Language of the Goddess* (San Francisco: HarperSanFrancisco, 1991), p. 321 (her concluding sentence).

17. See my discussion in *Reasons of the Heart* (New York: Macmillan, 1978; rpt. Notre Dame: University of Notre Dame Press, 1979), p. 1.

18. Hermann Broch, *The Death of Virgil*, trans. Jean Starr Untermeyer (San Francisco: North Point, 1983), p. 482 (the concluding words of the novel).

19. Ibid., p. 487.

20. See "Rainbow Dance" in the lyrics for "The Golden Key" in the appendix of my last book, *The Music of Time* (Notre Dame & London: University of Notre Dame Press, 1996).

21. Saint Augustine, *Confessions*, trans. Henry Chadwick (Oxford: Oxford University Press, 1991), p. 3.

22. See my book *The House of Wisdom* (San Francisco: Harper & Row, 1985; rpt. Notre Dame: University of Notre Dame Press, 1993) that I actually dedicated "to Ayasofya" (p. v).

23. See below "The Way Above" in the lyrics for "The Green Child."

24. T. S. Eliot, *Four Quartets* (San Diego, New York, London: Harcourt Brace, 1988), p. 10 (Eliot quotes the Greek from Diels's edition). His translation appears on p. 41 in line 129 of "The Dry Salvages": "And the way up is the way down, the way forward is the way back." My translation here is "The way above and the way below are one and the same."

25. Marcel Proust, *On Reading*, trans. John Sturrock (London and New York: Syrens/Penguin, 1994). See my discussion of this essay in *Love's Mind* (Notre Dame & London: University of Notre Dame Press, 1993), pp. 31–49.

26. 2 Samuel 6:14 (RSV).

27. See my description of this experience in *The Homing Spirit* (New York: Crossroad, 1987; Notre Dame: University of Notre Dame Press, 1997), p. 17.

28. Dag Hammarskjöld, "A Room of Quiet" (New York: The United Nations, 1971), the opening sentence.

29. See below "The Cloud of Forgetting" in the lyrics of "The Green Child."

30. Festugière, *Personal Religion among the Greeks*, p. 84.

31. For these phrases, "the cloud of unknowing" and "the cloud of forgetting," see *The Cloud of Unknowing and Other Works*, trans. Clifton Wolters (New York: Penguin, 1980), p. 66.

32. See Levinas's essay in Frans Jozef van Beeck, *Loving the Torah more than God?* (Chicago: Loyola University Press, 1989), pp. 35–40.

33. See below "Earth Dance" in the lyrics of "The Green Child."

The Way Below

1. Broch, *The Death of Virgil*, p. 20.
2. Ibid., p. 21.
3. Ibid., p. 7 (my translation). Cf. Dante, *Inferno* 34:133–39 in Paget Toynbee, *Le Opere di Dante Alighieri* (Oxford: Oxford University Press, 1924), p. 51.
4. Numbers 6:24–26 (RSV).
5. See above, "Setting Out," note 24.
6. Broch, *The Death of Virgil*, pp. 38–39.
7. Tolkien, *The Lord of the Rings*, p. 739.
8. See my discussion of the four cycles of story in *The Peace of the Present* (Notre Dame and London: University of Notre Dame Press, 1991), pp. 71–72.
9. See my discussion of Geronimo and Augustine in *Time and Myth* (Garden City, N.Y.: Doubleday, 1973; rpt. Notre Dame: University of Notre Dame Press, 1975), pp. 49–50.
10. Heidegger, *The Concept of Time*, p. 11E.
11. See my discussion of this saying of Heraclitus in *The Reasons of the Heart*, p. 92.
12. Tolkien, *The Lord of the Rings*, p. 292 and p. 721.
13. Paul Flohr, "The Road to I and Thou" in *Texts and Responses, Studies Presented to Nahum N. Glatzer*, ed. Michael Fishbane and Paul Flohr (Leiden: Brill, 1975), pp. 201–25.
14. Festugière, *Personal Religion among the Greeks*, pp. 53–67.
15. I have a little Oxford New Testament and Psalms "with the Harmony of the Gospels" as it says on the title page. It is in the King James Version, but no author of the Harmony is named and no date of publication is given, and the Harmony of the Gospels occupies only the last fifteen pages of the little volume.
16. Miguel de Cervantes, *Don Quijote*, trans. Burton Raffel (New York: Norton, 1995), p. 27.

17. Broch, *The Death of Virgil*, p. 63.

18. See my discussion of "God is vulnerable" in *The Church of the Poor Devil* (New York: Macmillan, 1982; rpt. Notre Dame: University of Notre Dame Press, 1983), p. 111.

19. Wilhelm Grimm and Maurice Sendak (illustrations), *Dear Mili* (New York: Farrar, Straus & Giroux, 1988) (pages not numbered).

20. Jacob and Wilhelm Grimm, *Grimm's Fairy Tales* (New York: Penguin, 1995) (nine stories: translator not named), p. 1.

21. Leonardo da Vinci, *Treatise on Painting* as quoted in E. H. Gombrich, *Shadows* (London: National Gallery distributed by Yale University Press, 1995), p. 20.

22. Martin Buber, *The Way of Man* (Secaucus, N.J.: Citadel, 1966), p. 18.

23. Gombrich, *Shadows*, p. 21.

24. *George MacDonald: An Anthology*, ed. C. S. Lewis (New York: Macmillan, 1978), p. 109.

25. Marguerite Yourcenar, *A Blue Tale*, trans. Alberto Manguel (Chicago: University of Chicago Press, 1995), p. 16.

26. Broch, *The Death of Virgil*, pp. 157–58 (this passage is written in capitals).

27. Rainer Maria Rilke, *Stories of God*, trans. M. D. Herter Norton (New York: Norton, 1963), p. 29.

28. Jacques Lacan quoted by William J. Richardson in his article "Like Straw: Religion and Psychoanalysis" in P. J. M. van Tongeren, ed., *Eros and Eris* (printed in the Netherlands: Kluwer Academic Publishers, 1992), p. 93.

29. Tolkien, *The Lord of the Rings*, p. 957.

30. Ibid., p. 739.

31. Michael Polanyi, *The Tacit Dimension* (Garden City, N.Y.: Anchor Doubleday, 1966), pp. 13–19. See my discussion in *Love's Mind*, pp. 60–63.

32. Shakespeare, *Henry IV*, Part 1, act 2, scene 4, line 359.

33. See my discussion in *Love's Mind*, pp. 86–87, of the saying in Malebranche and of Benjamin and Celan on its meaning.

34. See above, note 28.

35. Tolstoy, "The Death of Ivan Ilych" in Charles Neider, ed., *Tolstoy's Tales of Courage and Conflict* (Garden City, N.Y.: Hanover, 1958), p. 410.

36. See my comparison on Eckhart and Heidegger on "letting be" in *The Peace of the Present*, p. 18.

37. Heidegger, *Discourse on Thinking*, trans. John M. Anderson and E. Hans Freund, (New York: Harper & Row, 1966), p. 55.

38. See Gilbert Keith Chesterton, *Saint Francis of Assisi* (New York: Doran, 1924), pp. 19–24, and *Saint Thomas Aquinas* (New York: Doubleday, 1956), pp. 120–43 on "The Real Life of Saint Thomas."

39. See my *City of the Gods* (New York: Macmillan, 1965; rpt. Notre Dame: University of Notre Dame Press, 1978), p. v and p. 217.

40. These four sentences become chapter titles in my *House of Wisdom*, "Things are meant," p. 59; "There are signs," p. 80; "The heart speaks," p. 94; and "There is a way," p. 118.

41. See the preface to my last book, *The Music of Time*.

42. 1 Peter 3:11 (KJ).

43. Proust, *On Reading*, p. 55.

44. Ibid., p. 27.

45. Cervantes, *Don Quijote* (trans. Raffel), p. 10.

46. Broch, *The Death of Virgil*, p. 43.

47. Albert Bates Lord, *The Singer Resumes the Tale*, ed. Mary Louise Lord (Ithaca and London: Cornell University Press, 1995).

48. Ibid., p. xii (his wife's words).

49. Gerard Manley Hopkins, "Poetry and Verse" in *Hopkins*, ed. Peter Washington (New York: Knopf, 1995), p. 124.

50. Broch, *The Death of Virgil*, p. 376.

51. Richardson, "Like Straw," p. 93.

52. Thomas à Kempis, *The Imitation of Christ*, trans. Leo Sherley-Price (Baltimore: Penguin, 1952), p. 48 (Book 1, chapter 19).

53. Lord, *The Singer Resumes the Tale*, pp. 48–49.

54. Tolkien, *The Lord of the Rings*, p. 739.

55. Lord, *The Singer Resumes the Tale*, p. 49.

56. Ibid., p. 62.

57. A *Spinoza Reader*, ed. and trans. Edwin Curley (Princeton, N.J.: Princeton University Press, 1994), pp. 197 and 244.

58. Ibid., p. 253 (Book 5, Proposition 15).

59. See my discussion of this phrase in *Peace of the Present*, p. 15. See below, note 130.

60. See Ron Paquin and Robert Doherty, *Not First in Nobody's Heart* (Ames, Iowa: Iowa University Press, 1992). See my discussion in *Love's Mind*, p. 96.

61. Spinoza, *Ethics*, Book 3, Definition 6 in *A Spinoza Reader*. pp. 189–90.

62. Ibid., p. 188 (Definitions 2 and 3).

63. Reiner Schurmann, *Meister Eckhart* (Bloomington and London: Indiana University Press, 1978), p. xiv.

64. Jeremiah 3:13 (RSV).

65. *Hopkins*, pp. 72, 68, 69, 71, 74, 76.

66. Ibid., p. 19.

67. Thornton Wilder, *The Woman of Andros* (New York: Boni, 1930), p. 161.

68. Paul Celan, *Collected Prose*, trans. Rosemarie Waldrop (Manchester, U.K.: Carcanet, 1986), pp. 49–50.

69. Heidegger, *Discourse on Thinking*, p. 55.

70. *Hopkins*, p. 76.

71. "Everyman" in *Earlier English Drama*, ed. F. J. Tickner (London and Edinburgh: Nelson, 1926), p. 240.

72. John 1:5 in KJ.

73. John 1:5 in RSV.

74. Broch, *The Death of Virgil*, p. 151 (and see also p. 262).

75. Cervantes, *Don Quijote* (Raffel), p. 468.

76. Lacan as quoted by Slavoj Zizek, *Looking Awry* (Cambridge, Mass., and London: MIT Press, 1991), p. 48.

77. Tolstoy as quoted by Max Gorky, *Reminiscences of Tolstoy, Chekhov, and Andreev*, trans. by Katherine Mansfield, S.S. Koteliansky, and Leonard Woolf (London: Hogarth, 1948), p. 23.

78. Tolkien, *The Lord of the Rings*, p. 76.

79. Festugière, *Personal Religion among the Greeks*, p. 139.

80. Tolkien, *The Lord of the Rings*, p. 76.

81. Ibid., pp. 86–87.

82. George Steiner, *Real Presences* (Chicago: Chicago University Press, 1989).

83. See Festugière, *Personal Religion among the Greeks*, chapters 1, 5, and 6 on "popular piety," and 2, 7, and 8 on "reflective piety."

84. See Arthur J. Arberry, *The Koran Interpreted* (Oxford and New York: Oxford University Press, 1964), his preface and especially the last paragraph of his preface, pp. xii–xiii.

85. Isaiah 7:14 in Matthew 1:23 (KJ).

86. Tolkien, *The Lord of the Rings*, p. 980.

87. Ibid., pp. 325–26.

88. Heidegger as quoted in Schurmann, *Meister Eckhart*, p. vii (epigraph).

89. Tolkien, *The Lord of the Rings*, pp. 292 and 293.

90. Kathleen Norris, *Dakota* (New York: Ticknor & Fields, 1993), p. 102.

91. Plotinus, *Enneads* 6:9 in A. H. Armstrong, trans., *Plotinus*, vol. 7 (Cambridge, Mass.: Harvard University Press, 1988), p. 344 (*monos pros monon*). Armstrong translates "in solitude to the solitary" (p. 345).

92. Broch, *The Death of Virgil*, pp. 250–51.

93. Plato, *Republic* 509, trans. B. Jowett (New York: Random House/Modern Library, n.d.), pp. 249–50.

94. See Heidegger, *Being and Time*, trans. John Macquarrie and Edward Robinson (London: SCM, 1962), p. 47 on *ousia* as "presence" as in *parousia*.

95. Aristotle, *Nicomachean Ethics* 1158a, trans. H. Rackham (London and New York: Putnam/Heinemann, 1926), p. 475.

96. Freud quoted by Ernest Jones, *The Life and Work of Sigmund Freud*, vol. 2 (New York: Basic Books, 1955), p. 421.

97. Tolkien, *The Lord of the Rings*, p. 427.

98. Ibid., p. 981.

99. Ibid., p. 1011.

100. Ibid., p. 1062.

101. Freud, *Beyond the Pleasure Principle*, trans. C. J. M. Hubback (London: Hogarth, 1948), p. 32.

102. Tolkien, *The Lord of the Rings*, pp. 1010–11.

103. Festugière, *Personal Religion among the Greeks*, pp. 58–59.

104. Patricia A. McKillip, *The Book of Atrix Wolfe* (New York: Ace, 1995), p. 252.

105. George MacDonald, *Proving the Unseen*, ed. William J. Petersen (New York: Ballantine, 1989).

106. Andrei Tarkovsky, *Andrei Rublev*, trans. Kitty Hunter Blair (London and Boston: Faber & Faber, 1991), p. 129.

107. Broch, *The Death of Virgil*, p. 482.

108. Schurmann, *Meister Eckhart*, p. 192.

109. See my conversation with David Daube in *Peace of the Present*, pp. 93–95.

110. See "The Word at the End" in my last book, *The Music of Time*.

111. From the Bach Cantata. See my *House of Wisdom*, p. 3.

112. John G. Neihardt, *Black Elk Speaks* (Lincoln: University of Nebraska Press, 1961), pp. 1–2.

113. Ibid., p. 29.

114. Heidegger, "The Pathway," trans. Thomas F. O'Meara in *Listening* (Dubuque, Iowa: Aquinas Institute), Spring 1967, p. 7. (I've modified the translation slightly, using the German text on p. 6).

115. Ibid., p. 9 (cf. German on p. 8).

116. Heidegger, *Discourse on Thinking*, p. 55.

117. William Morris, vol. 2 of *The Well at the World's End* in vol. 19 of *The Collected Works of William Morris* (London: Longmans, 1913), p. 37.

118. See my discussion of this sentence in *The Reasons of the Heart*, pp. 94 and 111.

119. Heidegger, "The Pathway," p. 7.

120. Freud, *Beyond the Pleasure Principle*, p. 24.

121. Buber, *I and Thou*, trans. Ronald Gregor Smith (New York: Scribner's, 1958), p. 12.

122. Patricia A. McKillip, *The Cygnet and the Firebird* (New York: Ace, 1993), p. 302.

123. Buber, *I and Thou*, p. 3.

124. 1 Kings 3:5 and 9 (RSV).

125. *Jerusalem Bible* (New York: Doubleday, 1966), p. 422.

126. Buber, *I and Thou*, p. 6.

127. Ibid., p. 85.

128. John 10:30 (RSV).

129. This is my translation of "L'absence est a l'amour ce qu'est au feu le vent. Il eteint le petit, il allume le grand" in Roger de Bussy-Rabutin, "Maximes d'amour" at the end of his *Histoire amoureuse des Gaules* (Paris: Livre Club du Libraire, 1962), p. 172.

130. Swami Muktananda, *Getting Rid of What You Haven't Got* (Oakland, Calif.: S.Y.D.A. Foundation, 1978).

The Way Above

1. Abraham Pais names his biography of Einstein after this saying, "*Subtle is the Lord . . .*" (New York: Oxford University Press, 1982).

2. Plato, *The Symposium on Love*, trans. Percy Bysshe Shelley (New York: Peter Pauper, n.d.), p. 51.

3. John 21:15–17. See my discussion in *Peace of the Present*, p. 87.

4. Plato, *Symposium* (Shelley), p. 64.

5. Immanuel Kant, *Critique of Pure Reason*, trans. Norman Kemp Smith (London: Macmillan, 1963), p. 93. See my *Homing Spirit*, p. 59.

6. Pais, "*Subtle is the Lord . . .*," p. vi.

7. See my *House of Wisdom*, especially the second chapter.

8. Wisdom of Solomon 7:22–23.

9. Vladmir Solovyov, "Three Meetings," trans. Ralph Koprince in *The Silver Age of Russian Culture*, ed. Carl and Ellendea Proffer (Ann Arbor, Mich.: Ardis, 1979), pp. 128 and 134.

10. In my *Love's Mind*, pp. 125–26.

11. See my *House of Wisdom*, p. 25, and *Love's Mind*, p. 48.

12. Wisdom of Solomon 8:2 (RSV).

13. John 3:8 (RSV).

14. George MacDonald, *At the Back of the North Wind* (New York: Penguin, 1994). p. 80.

15. Ibid., p. 82.

16. Ibid., p. 83.

17. Ibid., p. 92.

18. Ibid., pp. 92–93.

19. Ibid., p. 83.

20. Edward Conze, *Buddhist Wisdom Books* (London: Allen & Unwin, 1958), p. 77 and pp. 101–102.

21. See my discussion in *The City of the Gods*, p. 105.

22. Luke 7:35 and Matthew 11:19 (RSV).

23. Luke 11:49 (RSV).

24. Matthew 23:34.

25. 1 Corinthians 1:24.

26. See my *Peace of the Present*, p. 94.

27. MacDonald, *At the Back of the North Wind*, p. 89.

28. John 1:8 (RSV).

29. Gerard Manley Hopkins, in his essay "Poetry and Verse" in *Hopkins*, ed. Peter Washington (New York: Knopf, 1995), p. 124.

30. MacDonald, *At the Back of the North Wind*, p. 325 and pp. 327–28.

31. Robert A. Johnson, *Lying with the Heavenly Woman* (San Francisco: HarperSanFrancisco, 1994), p. 54.

32. MacDonald, *At the Back of the North Wind*, p. 83.

33. Wisdom of Solomon 9:4 (RSV) (9:1–6, 9–11 are the verses used in The Liturgy of Hours).

34. See my *House of Wisdom*, p. 123 and p. 153.

35. See my discussion in *The Peace of the Present*, p. 18.

36. I give a literal translation with the Spanish in *The Homing Spirit*, p. 80.

37. Wisdom of Solomon 9:11 (RSV).

38. Plato, *Symposium* (Shelley), pp. 56, 57, and 59.

39. Ludwig Wittgenstein, *Tractatus Logico-Philosophicus*, trans. D. F. Pears and B. F. McGuinness (London: Routledge & Kegan Paul, 1974), p. 149 (# 6.45).

40. Spinoza, Letter 64 in *Spinoza Reader*, p. 272.

41. Wittgenstein, *Tractatus*, p. 149 (## 6.45 and 6.44).

42. See my discussion in *The House of Wisdom*, p. 3.

43. Flannery O'Connor, *Mystery and Manners* (New York: Farrar, Straus & Giroux, 1962), p. 226. See my *Church of the Poor Devil*, p. 102.

44. Teilhard de Chardin, *The Divine Milieu*, ed. Bernard Wall (New York: Harper & Row, 1965), pp. 6–7 (table of contents).

45. O'Connor, *Mystery and Manners*, p. 223.

46. Ivar Ekeland, *Mathematics and the Unexpected* (Chicago: University of Chicago Press, 1988), pp. 121–23 (concluding words).

47. Gustave Flaubert, *La tentation de saint Antoine* (Paris: Garnier-Flammerion, 1967), p. 252 (my translation).

48. O'Connor, *Mystery and Manners*, p. 227.

49. Wilfrid Mellers in *The Messiaen Companion*, ed. Peter Hill (Portland, Ore.: Amadeus, 1995), p. 222.

50. See below "A Note on the Dante-Riemann Universe."

51. Robert Osserman, *Poetry of the Universe* (New York: Doubleday, 1995), p. 194.

52. Wittgenstein, *Tractatus*, p. 147 (#6.4311).

53. Peter Washington, ed., *Donne* (New York: Knopf, 1995), p. 163.

54. Brian Stock, *Augustine the Reader* (Cambridge, Mass.: Harvard University Press, 1996).

55. On the "event horizon" see Stephen Hawking and Roger Penrose, *The Nature of Space and Time* (Princeton, N.J.: Princeton University Press, 1996), pp. 87–88, 94–95, 97–99, 103, and 121–22. The term is used also of the "event horizon" of a "black hole." See the diagrams of such a horizon there on pp. 22–23, 28, 38, 42, and 45.

56. Osserman, *Poetry of the Universe*, p. 90 (see note on p. 189).

57. Dante, *Paradiso*, Canto 28, trans. P. H. Wicksteed (New York: Dutton, 1912), pp. 338–47.

58. See my *Way of All the Earth* (New York: Macmillan, 1972; rpt. Notre Dame: University of Notre Dame Press, 1978), p. 232 (concluding paragraph).

59. Bernhard Riemann, "On the Hypotheses which lie at the Bases of Geometry" trans. by William Kingdon Clifford in Clifford's *Mathematical Papers* (London: Macmillan, 1882), pp. 55–71 (esp. pp. 67–68 on space as unbounded yet finite).

60. Dante, *Paradiso* 29.11–12 (Toynbee, p. 145).

61. Arthur Weisberg, *Performing Twentieth-Century Music* (New Haven, Conn.: Yale University Press, 1993), p. 1.

62. Augustine, *Confessions*, trans. Henry Chadwick (Oxford: Oxford University Press, 1991), pp. 170–71 (Book 9, chapter 10).

63. See Chadwick's introduction to Augustine's *Confessions*, p. xxii on the Psalms Augustine is using (numbered according to the Latin versions), and see Igor Stravinsky, *Symphony of Psalms* (London: Boosey & Hawkes, 1948), page facing p. 1 on those Stravinsky is using (also numbered according to the Latin versions).

64. Franz Kafka, *The Great Wall of China*, trans. Willa and Edwin Muir (New York: Schocken, 1946), p. 306 (#101), "Our relation to our fellow men is that of prayer, our relation to ourselves that of effort." I take the word "striving" from Nahum Glatzer's translation of the same passage in his *Language of Faith* (New York: Schocken, 1967), p. 35.

65. Augustine, *Confessions* 10.14 (Chadwick, p. 191).

66. See Night Prayer after Evening Prayer II on Sundays in *The Liturgy of the Hours* (New York: Catholic Book Publishing, 1975), vol. 1, p. 1173.

67. Pierre Hadot, *Plotinus or the Simplicity of Vision*, trans. Michael Chase (Chicago: University of Chicago, 1993), p. 63.

68. Roy Campbell, *Poems of St. John of the Cross* (London: Harvill, 1953), p. 10 (Spanish). Campbell translates "that lucky night," p. 11. See also my translation of the poem in *Love's Mind*, pp. 100–101.

69. Augustine, *Confessions* 8.12 (Chadwick, p. 153) (Romans 13:13–14).

70. Psalm 131:2 (RSV).
71. Hadot, *Plotinus*, p. 40.
72. Heidegger, *The Concept of Time*, p. 12E.
73. John 17:23 (RSV).
74. Hadot, *Plotinus*, p. 3.
75. See my discussion of this saying of Hillel's in *The Homing Spirit*, p. 83.
76. John 17:24 (RSV).
77. Hadot, *Plotinus*, p. 45.
78. Ibid., p. 30.
79. Ibid., p. 40.
80. Ibid., p. 41.
81. See my discussion in *The Peace of the Present*, p. 30.
82. *The Book of Common Prayer 1559*, ed. John E. Booty (Charlottesville: University of Virginia Press, 1976), p. 291.
83. Tolkien, *The Lord of the Rings*, pp. 86–87.
84. Psalm 39:7 in *The Liturgy of the Hours*, vol. 1, p. 853.
85. Paul Griffiths, *Stravinsky* (New York: Schirmer, 1993), p. 102.
86. Concluding words of my song "In the Lost Hills" in *Love's Mind*, p. 126.
87. Tolkien, *The Adventures of Tom Bombadil*, p. 9.
88. Hadot, *Plotinus*, p. 100 (quoting Pascal, *pensee* #211 in the Brunschvicg edition).
89. See my discussion in *The City of the Gods*, p. 217.
90. See my discussion in *The Reasons of the Heart*, p. 92.
91. See my discussion in *The Homing Spirit*, p. 69.
92. T. E. Lawrence, *Seven Pillars of Wisdom* (Garden City, N.J.: Doubleday, 1935), pp. 355–56. See my *Reasons of the Heart*, p. 1.
93. Proverbs 9:1 (RSV).
94. Dante, *Paradiso* 33:145 (Paget Toynbee, p. 135). This is the literal translation, but see below for a freer translation in blank verse.
95. Heinrich von Kleist, "On the Marionette Theatre" trans. Idris Parry in *Essays on Dolls* (London: Syrens/Penguin, 1994), p. 3.

96. 2 Samuel 6:14 (RSV).

97. Kleist, "On the Marionette Theatre," p. 7.

98. T. S. Eliot, *Four Quartets* (New York: Harcourt Brace, 1988), p. 15 ("Burnt Norton," line 62).

99. Michel Serres, *Genesis*, trans. by Genevieve James and James Nielson (Ann Arbor, Mich.: University of Michigan Press, 1995), p. 1.

100. Martin Buber, *Ecstatic Confessions*, ed. by Paul Mendes-Flohr, trans. by Esther Cameron (San Francisco: Harper & Row, 1985), p. 11.

101. Serres, *Genesis*, pp. 9–26.

102. Edward Lorenz, *The Essence of Chaos* (Seattle: University of Washington Press, 1993), pp. 181–84.

103. Serres, *Genesis*, p. 13.

104. 1 Kings 19:11–12 (RSV).

105. John Cage, *Silence* (Hanover, N.H.: Wesleyan, 1973), p. 3.

106. Honore de Balzac, *Gillette or the Unknown Masterpiece*, trans. by Anthony Rudolf (London: Menard, 1988), p. 26.

107. Ibid., p. 30.

108. Ibid., p. 31.

109. Serres, *Genesis*, p. 37.

110. Ibid., pp. 49–80.

111. Balzac, *Gillette*, p. 30.

112. Lorenz, *The Essence of Chaos*, p. 50.

113. Serres, *Genesis*, pp. 115–22.

114. Ibid., p. 138.

115. Jorge Luis Borges, "The Meeting in a Dream" in his *Other Inquisitions*, trans. by Ruth L. C. Simms (New York: Washington Square, 1966), pp. 101ff.

116. Kleist, "On the Marionette Theatre," p. 12.

117. Arnold Schoenberg, *Verklärte Nacht and Pierrot Lunaire* (New York: Dover, 1994), p. 54 (trans. by Stanley Applebaum).

118. Kleist, "On the Marionette Theatre," p. 6.

119. Dante, *Paradiso* 33:144–45 (Toynbee, p. 153) (my trans.).

The Mystic Road of Love

1. Jack Kerouac, *On the Road* (New York: Penguin, 1991).
2. *Goethe's Fairy Tale of the Green Snake and the Beautiful Lily*, trans. Donald MacLean (Grand Rapids, Mich.: Phanes, 1993).
3. See Raymond Lister, *The Paintings of William Blake* (Cambridge: Cambridge University Press, 1991), # 20 (it is in the Victoria and Albert Museum in London).
4. *Goethe's Fairy Tale*, p. 30.
5. Victor Pellevin, *The Yellow Arrow*, trans. Andrew Bromfield (New York: New Directions, 1996), p. 8.
6. Ibid., p. 92.
7. Heidegger, *Being and Time*, trans. John Macquarrie and Edward Robinson (New York: Harper & Row, 1962), p. 19.
8. *Goethe's Fairy Tale*, p. 24 (she hears it from the old woman), p. 26 (from the Green Snake), p. 34 (from the old man), but p. 17 (it is first said by the old man when the snake whispers in his ear).
9. Ibid., p. 32.
10. Tolkien, *The Lord of the Rings*, p. 498.
11. Reiner Schurmann, *Meister Eckhart* (Bloomington: Indiana University Press, 1978), p. 205.
12. John 1:1–5 (RSV).
13. Helen Luke, "Choice in *The Lord of the Rings*" (Apple Farm Group Discussions: Three Rivers, Michigan) (no date), p. 16. This is an unpublished essay of Helen's. But before she died I asked her if I could quote from it and she gave me permission.
14. Dag Hammarskjold, *Markings*, trans. Leif Sjoberg and W. H. Auden (New York: Knopf, 1964), p. 89.
15. See below "Letting Go" in the lyrics of "The Green Child." I am using the image of a bird held by a thread from "The Ascent of Mount Carmel." See Kieran Kavanaugh and Otilio Rodriguez, *Collected Works of St. John of the Cross* (Washington, DC: ICS, 1979), p. 97.
16. Helen Luke, "Choice," p. 16.
17. Robertson Davies, *Fifth Business* (Toronto: Macmillan, 1970), p. 305. See my discussion in *The Homing Spirit*, p. 42.

18. John 2:24–25 (RSV).

19. Helen Luke, "Choice," p. 17.

20. John 15:16 (RSV).

21. Tolkien, *The Lord of the Rings*, p. 288.

22. Helen Waddell, *Poetry in the Dark Ages* (New York: Barnes & Noble, 1948, rpt. 1960).

23. Seamus Heaney, *Crediting Poetry* (his Nobel Lecture) (New York: Farrar, Straus Giroux, 1996), p. 10 and pp. 33–34.

24. Meister Eckhart quoted by David Applebaum in the epigraph to his book, *The Vision of Kant* (Rockport, Mass.: Element, 1995).

25. Pelevin, *The Yellow Arrow*, p. 36.

26. Helen Waddell, *The Desert Fathers* (London: Constable, 1936), pp. 28–29, quoted in James Hillman, *The Thought of the Heart* (Eranos Lecture) (Dallas: Spring Pbns., 1981), p. 43.

27. Helen Waddell, *Poetry in the Dark Ages*, p. 23. See my discussion in *Love's Mind*, p. 95.

28. Wallace Stevens quoted in Hillman, *The Thought of the Heart*, p. 42. See below, note 30.

29. Meister Eckhart quoted by William James, *The Varieties of Religious Experience* (New York: Mentor, 1958), p. 320. See my discussion in *The Music of Time*, p. 25.

30. Wallace Stevens, "Notes toward a Supreme Fiction" in *Stevens*, poems selected by Helen Vendler (New York: Knopf, 1993), p. 162.

31. See William Morris, *The Well at the World's End* (New York: Ballantine, 1977), p. 401 where Morris has these words inscribed on the well: "Ye who have come a long way to look upon me, drink of me, if ye deem that ye be strong enough in desire to bear length of days: or else drink not; but tell your friends and the kindreds of the earth how ye have seen a great marvel." See below my lyrics for "The Well at the World's End" based on his story.

A Note on the Dante-Riemann Universe

1. T. S. Eliot, *Four Quartets* (New York: Harcourt Brace Jovanovich, 1988), p. 15 (Burnt Norton, line 62). On the Dante-Riemann

universe see Robert Osserman, *Poetry of the Universe* (New York: Doubleday/Anchor, 1995), pp. 89–92.

2. See J. S. Bell, *Speakable and Unspeakable in Quantum Mechanics* (Cambridge: Cambridge University Press, 1987), pp. 93–99 and 127–37 and 193 (critique of "the world wave function" and "the many worlds interpretation"). And see Stephen Hawking and Roger Penrose, *The Nature of Space and Time* (Princeton: Princeton University Press, 1996), p. 81 (Hawking on "the wave function of the universe") and p. 84 (a function of the radius of the universe).

3. Max Jacob, *The Dice Cup*, ed. Michael Brownstein (New York: State University of New York Press, 1979), p. 5 (from preface written in 1916).

4. See William Kingdon Clifford, *Mathematical Papers* (Bronx, N.Y.: Chelsea, 1968) (reprint of first edition of 1882). See Clifford's own "Space-Theory of Matter" on pp. 21–22.

5. Judging from the mass parameter in the time-independent Schrödinger equation, $8\pi^2 m(E - U)/h^2$ equivalent to $(2\pi/\lambda)^2$, I would expect $x_5 = \lambda/2\pi = h/2\pi mv$. Looking for a relativistic equation where mass figures as a fifth term alongside the four dimensions of space and time, I think of the Klein-Gordon wave equation and of the Dirac wave equation. Judging from the Klein-Gordon equation, I would expect $x_5 = h/2\pi mc$, which is the Compton wavelength, but judging from the Dirac equation, I would expect $x_5 = ih/2\pi mc$, where i is $\sqrt{-1}$ and h is the Planck constant and c is the velocity of light. It is true, m in these wave equations is usually taken to be rest mass and is treated therefore as a constant, but if we take it instead to be relativistic mass, as in the DeBroglie formula, we can treat it as a variable.

6. Bernhard Riemann, Inaugural Lecture ("On the Hypotheses Which Lie at the Bases of Geometry") translated by Clifford in his *Mathematical Papers*, pp. 55–71 and especially p. 65 (Riemann's formula for the line element in curved space).

7. Abraham Pais, '*Subtle is the Lord . . .*', The Science and Life of Albert Einstein (Oxford: Oxford University Press, 1982), pp. 329–32 (on the fifth dimension and the Kaluza-Klein unified field theory), and p. 332 (Klein quoted on quantum scale of x_5).

8. Albert Einstein, *The Meaning of Relativity* (Princeton: Princeton University Press, 1956), pp. 116–17.

9. See Roger Penrose on the idea of a decay of the wave function in a gravitational field ("the objective reduction of the wave function" referred to below in note 10) with decay time $T = h/2\pi E$.

10. The "many-worlds interpretation" arises from assuming that all possibilities included in the wave function ψ are realized, and since they are incompatible alternatives, realized in different worlds. But taking the wave function ψ as a function not only of space and time but also of matter, as we are doing here, we can suppose instead of the many worlds something like "the objective reduction of the wave function" that Roger Penrose envisions in Hawking and Penrose, *The Nature of Space and Time*, pp. 70–72. See also Penrose, *The Large, the Small and the Human Mind* (Cambridge: Cambridge University Press, 1997), pp. 83–87.

Index

forgiveness: in friendship, 93;
relationship to time in the
Bible, 96
"forsaking all others," in the
marriage vows, 96
Four Quartets (Eliot), 9–10
fourth dimension, 140
freedom, 35–36, 116; images of, 33–34
Freud, Sigmund, 52, 53–54, 56–57,
64, 107
friendship, ix, 18, 48–50, 118;
Aristotle on, 53; divine, 49–50;
experience of, as stage in time
of loss or disappointment, 51,
53–55; the "I and thou" of,
64–65, 79; loss of, portrayal in
The Green Child song and
dance cycle, 125; Philia/love
as, x, 70, 90–99; real presences
found in, 44–45. *See also*
companionship
"Frodo's Dreme" ("The Sea Bell")
(Tolkien), 1–3
Frog Prince, The (Grimm), 20

Gate of Horn, 42–43, 46, 48
Gate of Ivory, 42–43, 46, 48
Gelassenheit. See letting be/letting
go
Genesis (Serres), 101–2, 103–4, 107
Genesis, Book of, story of
emergence and separation
of the human race, 16
Gerber, John, 123
Geronimo, story of, 16
Gimbutas, Marija, 5–6
Giono, Jean, 98–99

God
as enough, 92, 97
journey with (*see* journey[s],
with God in time)
love from and of and towards, 7,
43, 45, 47, 58, 70–71, 100
(*see also* love of God); as the
circle of love, 60–61; in
Lawrence's story, viii, 6, 57, 99,
120; Plato's vision of Good seen
in, 50–52; spoken of in the
Well at the World's End song
and dance cycle, 131
peace of, 14, 17
presence of (*see* presence of God)
relationship with, 4–6, 8, 12, 92;
"I and thou" as, 6, 19–20, 63,
66–67, 95, 116; praying for
peace of God in, 14
remembrance of, 24
repose of the heart in, 56
reunion with, 6, 8, 12, 16
seen as at center of an invisible
sphere, 88, 137
seen as vulnerable, 20–21
spoken of in the *Well at the
World's End* song and dance
cycle, 134, 136
telling us our story, prayer as
listening to, 32–34, 35,
36–37
trust in, 14
withdrawal and return, story of, 2,
15–16
Goddess, the, 5–6, 24
"God with us," 2, 47, 56, 58.
See also presence of God

Goethe, Johann Wolfgang von, 37,
94, 111–12, 113–14
Golden Key, The (MacDonald),
Dunne's musical
interpretation of, 7
Gombrich, E. H., 21–22
Good, the, 50–53
good and evil, knowledge of, 113;
as death-dealing wisdom, 112
Gorky, Max, 43
grace, 80, 100, 133
gravity, center of, 100–101;
connecting with center of
stillness, 109; spoken of in the
Well at the World's End song
and dance cycle, 133
Green Child, The (Read), song and
dance cycle based on, xi–xii, 1,
9, 11, 12, 80, 123, 125–30
"Green Snake and the Beautiful
Lily, The" (Goethe), 111–12,
113–14
Grimm's fairy tales: *Dear Mili*, 20;
The Frog Prince, 20

Hadot, Pierre, 92, 95–96, 98
Hagia Sophia (Ayasofya), ix, 9, 70,
72, 74
Hammarskjold, Dag, 57, 116
"Harmony of the Gospels, The," 19,
46, 47, 146n15
Hawking, Stephen, 138
healing, 3, 5, 8–9, 17–18; link with
timelessness, 56–57
Heaney, Seamus, 119
heart
"God and my heart weeping
together," 20

listening to one's own speak, 35,
62, 69
longing of the, shared in
friendship, 90
"reasons of the," 103
repose of in God, 56
restlessness: as "restless until it
rests in you," 10, 34, 52, 56, 102;
spoken of in the *Well at the
World's End* song and dance
cycle, 131–32
singing timelessness of the, 31
speaking, prayer as attention
to, 118
understanding, 65–66
heart's desire. *See* longing
heart speaks to heart, 19, 73, 76, 89,
97; spoken of in *The Green
Child* song and dance cycle,
125, 128; spoken of in the *Well
at the World's End* song and
dance cycle, 134
Heart Sutra, in Buddhism, 75–76,
79
Heidegger, Martin, 3–4, 17, 60, 61,
94; *Being and Time*, 1–2, 29,
113; on *Gelassenheit*, 27, 49, 62,
114
Heraclitus, 9–10, 14–15, 18, 98
Hillel, 95
Holocaust, the, Levinas's response
to, 12
Holy Wisdom. *See* Wisdom
hope, 22, 59–60, 92–93, 98–99, 107
combined with willingness, 21;
death approached with, 17–18
spoken of in *The Green Child*
song and dance cycle, 127–28

presence, 48, 52, 66–67, 95; eternal
life as living in the, 87, 91, 93;
God as total, 95–96; peace of,
87, 125; spoken of in *The Green
Child* song and dance cycle,
125, 126, 127; staying in the,
89–90. *See also* presence of
God
presence of God (the Shekinah),
vii, 36, 51–52, 60, 96, 102;
eternity as, 87, 89–90; "God
with us," 2, 47–48, 56, 58; Jesus
as "I am," 77; in loneliness,
40–41, 45; practice of, 100–101;
as relation, 67–68; soul of the
universe as a metaphor for, 86
primum mobile, 137
Proust, Marcel, 10, 27, 30–31
Proverbs, Book of, 99
Psalms, 91–92, 93, 96
psychoanalysis, feeling at end of, 24,
55

quantum theory, 137–40
Quartet for the End of Time
(Messiaen), 85–86

rainbow, as an image of love,
6–8, 69
Read, Herbert. *See Green Child,
The*
reading, and recollection, 27–31
real, the: encounter with, 32–33,
42–45, 50; integration of
with the symbolic and the
imaginary, 26–27; love as,
50–59

real presences, 45, 47
recollection (memories/y;
remembering), 4–5, 8–12, 14,
23–32
"reflective piety," 44, 46
relativity, theory of, 137–38, 140
remembering God (*dikhr Allah*), 14,
55–56
repetition, 56, 64–65
Republic, The (Plato), 50–51, 52
rest, in God, 56–57
restlessness of the heart, 10, 34, 52,
56, 102; spoken of in the *Well
at the World's End* song and
dance cycle, 131–32
reunion, 2, 4, 6, 15–17, 30, 107–8;
with other human beings, 8, 12,
15, 17–18, 30, 35
Revisions (Augustine), 4
rhythm, 89
Richardson, William, 24–25
riddle song, 33
Riemann, Bernhard, 88, 89, 137,
139; Dante-Riemann universe,
88, 137–41
Rilke, Rainer Maria, 24
road(s), viii, 1–2, 46, 111; not taken,
29, 126. *See also* journey(s);
mystic road of love
"Road Goes Ever On, The"
(Tolkien), 96
Romans 14:7–9, 2

sacrifice, role in Goethe's
"The Green Snake," 111
sadness (sorrow), 36–39, 131;
healing, 124, 127, 129

"unhoped-for, the," 18, 98, 113
universe: division into two spheres,
    88, 137; in Riemann's multi-
    dimensional geometry, 137
Untermeyer, Jean Starr, 6

Virgil, viii–ix, 9, 27, 42; Dante
    guided out of hell by, 6, 13–14;
    deathbed, 9, 24–25, 27, 41–42,
    60. See also Death of Virgil
vision, 89–90, 108; and a gain in
    sensibility, 84–85; of God, seen
    by Dante, 88; living in the
    simplicity of, 93; of repose in
    God for Plotinus, 94; shared
    in friendship, 90, 99
vulnerability: in coming from
    the human circle to solitude,
    46–47; of God, 20–21; to loss,
    67; to love and to sorrow, 20–21

Waddell, Helen, 119, 120
walking alone, 129; willingness for,
    96–97, 115–17, 127
"wandering joy," 61
wave function, 137–38, 139–40,
    160n5, 161nn9, 10
"Way Above," 9, 69–109, 114;
    readiness for, 68; spoken of in
    The Green Child song and
    dance cycle, 129
"Way Below," 9, 13–68, 114–16
"way forward," as "way back," 15–16
Well at the World's End, The
    (Morris), 63, 121; song and
    dance cycle based on, xi–xii,
    123–24, 131–36

wholeness, 3, 8–9, 21, 114
    in combination of willingness
        and hope, 17–18
    of love, 10, 12; spoken of in The
        Green Child song and dance
        cycle, 129–30
Wilder, Thornton, 38
willingness: combined with hope,
    17–18, 21; to walk alone, 96–97,
    115–17, 127
wisdom, 112, 113
Wisdom (Holy Wisdom), 72, 73;
    address to in the Liturgy of the
    Hours, 79–80; figure of,
    Ayasofya as (see Ayasofya, as
    figure); figure of in The Green
    Child song and dance cycle,
    125–26, 128; as guide for
    Dunne, 70–81, 104, 118–19;
    "I and thou" with, 74–77;
    Solovyov's encounters with,
    108; spoken of in the Well at
    the World's End song and
    dance cycle, 131, 132
Wisdom of Solomon, 72, 74, 79,
    80–81
Wittgenstein, Ludwig, 82, 87
Wolf, Maryanne, 123
Woman of Andros, The (Wilder), 38
word(s)
    always returning into
        silence, 20
    beyond speech, 59–68, 118
    real presences found in,
        44–45, 47
    reunion with music, 29–30, 103,
        105, 107, 108; in song and